Frontiers in Chinese Linguistics

Volume 1

Frontiers in Chinese Linguistics (FiCL) is a book series jointly published by Springer-Nature and Peking University Press. FiCL aims to publish original and innovative research outcome in the fast expanding and developing discipline of Chinese language sciences. FiCL welcomes submissions of proposals of the following types of books on issues related to Chinese language and linguistics: selection of post-conference papers from leading edge prestigious conferences and workshops; monograph on research with potential to open new frontiers; and outstanding dissertations dealing with new issues and new methodologies. FiCL volumes will be published by Springer with worldwide distribution and by Peking University Press in China. FiCL is the sister series of 语言学前沿, a prestigious book series published in Chinese by Peking University Press introducing new theories and new ideas in Chinese linguistics.

More information about this series at http://www.springer.com/series/15591

Jing Ding

A Lexical Semantic Study of Chinese Opposites

北京大学出版社
PEKING UNIVERSITY PRESS

Springer

Jing Ding
School of International Education
South China University of Technology
Guangzhou, Guangdong
China

ISSN 2522-5308 ISSN 2522-5316 (electronic)
Frontiers in Chinese Linguistics
ISBN 978-981-10-6183-7 ISBN 978-981-10-6184-4 (eBook)
https://doi.org/10.1007/978-981-10-6184-4

The print edition is not for sale in China Mainland. Customers from China Mainland please order the print book from: Peking University Press.

Library of Congress Control Number: 2017949125

Published by Peking University Press and Springer Nature in conjunction with the PolyU-PKU Research Center on Chinese Linguistics

Printed on acid-free paper

This Springer imprint is published by Springer Nature
The registered company is Springer Nature Singapore Pte Ltd.
The registered company address is: 152 Beach Road, #21-01/04 Gateway East, Singapore 189721, Singapore

Editorial Committee

Academic Advisory Committee

Preface of Frontiers in Chinese Linguistics

Frontiers in Chinese Linguistics (*FiCL*) is a book series jointly published by Springer Nature and Peking University Press. *FiCL* aims to publish original and innovative research outcomes in the fast expanding and developing discipline of Chinese language sciences. *FiCL* welcomes submissions of proposals of the following types of books on issues related to Chinese language and linguistics: selection of post-conference papers from leading-edge prestigious conferences and workshops, monograph on research with potential to open new frontiers and outstanding dissertation dealing with new issues and new methodologies. *FiCL* volumes will be published by Springer Nature with worldwide distribution and by Peking University Press in China.

FiCL is the sister series of 语言学前沿丛书, a prestigious book series published in Chinese by Peking University Press since 2000. The series introduces new theories and new ideas in Chinese Linguistics to the wide communities of linguists in China as well as Chinese linguists overseas. Since 2010, in order to bring a broader international perspective and impact, 语言学前沿丛书 has entered a collaborative publication agreement with the PolyU-PKU Joint Research Centre on Chinese Linguistics (RP2U2). Both parties work jointly to form the editorial board and academic advisory committee in order to ensure more rigorous academic review process as well as to facilitate introduction of interdisciplinary-pioneering topics to the series.

The collaboration with Springer Nature adds a third world-leading partner to this joint publication series. This new arrangement will allow the series to publish excellent monographs written in English as well as ensure that all publications are equally accessible in China and overseas. With the new arrangement, we also propose to introduce two new types of publications that were not published by 语言学前沿丛书 before. One type is the thematic collection of excellent papers from international conferences, for these papers typically represents the forefront of the field. The other is from the new initiative also started by Peking University Press and RP2U2 to select a Ph.D. thesis of the year on Chinese Linguistics through worldwide call and competition. The award-winning theses would also represent the newest breakthroughs in the field, and we plan to publish the excellent award-winning thesis of the year after review and revision.

Last but not the least, *FiCL* will be included in major international scientific indexes such as SCOPUS and Google Scholar. With the competition in the field, effective indexing and sharing is essential to the reputation of the publication as well as authors whose theses are published in the series. Your contribution as author, reviewer, reader, and submitter is essential to the success of this book series.

Kowloon, Hong Kong
Beijing, China
February 2017

Chu-Ren Huang
Rui Guo

Acknowledgements

My deepest gratitude belongs to my supervisor, Prof. Huang Chu-Ren. Without his guidance and support, this work can never be finished. I also appreciate the discussions with our teammates, especially Xu Hongzhi, Liu Ming, and Anna Laszlo. Their words inspired me a lot in many ways. The suggestions from anonymous reviewers push me to improve the work in details. I owe them many thanks. My dearest editors, Rebecca and Hannah from Springer Publishing Company, and Li Ling from Peking University Press, offer me great patience and endless help. I sincerely thank them and everyone working for this book but unknown to me. In the end, I would like to thank my family and friends, for encouraging me all along the way.

Any mistakes in this book, of course, are mine. And I would be more than grateful to any discussions for improvements, corrections, questions, or comments.

Contents

List of Figures

List of Tables

Abstract

Previous studies on opposites focused on its sub-type classification such as antonym (or, gradable opposite), complementary (or, ungradable opposite), and converse (or, relational opposite) but are not enough to clarify the differences among the three sub-types. Besides, the behaviors of opposites in natural language has not been observed and discussed yet. Therefore, these two questions trigger our work on the topic of opposites.

With a large-scale corpus, this work focuses on Chinese opposites, a relatively poorly explored language in this area, as the experimental object, and has finished three studies on the behaviors of the three main sub-types, from character-based constructions to free-constrained contexts.

The first study focuses on the opposite pairings in constructions from bi-syllabic to quad-syllabic. We discuss the semantic functions of these pairings under different structures. For practical usages and explore the determining principles in opposite member order. Our findings suggest that Pollyanna principle is not enough to explain all the Chinese data. Prosodic principle and temporal order may influence the opposite order in constructions.

The second study is an extensional work of the first one. Syntactic frames are used to extract the opposite pairings' co-occurrence in discourse. Result of it shows the differences among the three sub-types of opposites in discourse function distribution and that among Chinese, English, and Japanese. Moreover, we use frequency and frame distribution to define canonical opposite pairings and find that Chinese data challenges the hypothesis in previous researches.

In study 2, we notice that negation frames only take a small percentage in Chinese result. In order to see the relation between negation and opposites, we design study 3. We use negation frames to trigger out pairings in free-constrained context. Result clearly shows that, rather than opposites, other semantic relations also occur in these frames. It suggests that, words in negation frames are not necessary to be opposites.

In sum, the three studies cover the most discussed topics in previous studies about opposite relation. This work is meaningful in the theoretical discussion on semantic relations, as well as in the practical resource building for Information Extraction as general.

Chapter 1
Introduction

1.1 Motivations

The **opposites**, also known as the oppositions, are generally defined as the words which have contrast meanings. It is easy for language users to response to questions like: "What is the opposite of X?" However, it is hard to clarify how the opposites are used in natural language and why they are used in this way. Moreover, the differences of how we use the three main sub-types of opposites, that is, complementary (or, ungradable opposites), antonym (or, gradable opposites) and converse (or, relational opposites) (Lyons 1968; Cruse 1986, among others), are remained unclear. Besides, recent researches (Murphy 2003, among others) suggest that, for each conceptual opposite pair, there might be one canonical pairing. Some corpus-based studies (Jones 2002, among others) support this hypothesis but have limitation on the data. It seems that the lexical semantic relation of opposites has been theoretically discussed for a long time but has not been practically explored yet. Chinese opposites, which are not completely studied in previous literatures, call for a deep research. At the same time, the comparison between Chinese and other languages, like English, would also be very interesting.

1.2 Research Questions

In this work the two main questions we want to be answered are: (1) how are opposites used in Chinese; and, (2) how are the three sub-types of opposites (complementary, antonym and converse) used differently in Chinese?

In order to uncover the facts, we design three related studies on one large scale corpus. Our observation on Chinese opposites starts from morphological level (from bi-syllabic to quad-syllabic constructions) to discourse level (via syntactic frames), to trace how opposites are used in natural language. After that, a third

J. Ding, *A Lexical Semantic Study of Chinese Opposites*,
Frontiers in Chinese Linguistics 1, https://doi.org/10.1007/978-981-10-6184-4_1

study is added for an interesting finding we have in study 2, that is, negation frames take quite a small percentage in opposite co-occurrence discourse. It further explains the relation between negation and opposites.

1.3 Organization of Chapters

This work is organized as follow:

Chapter 1 is an overview of the whole work. It introduces the research background and the contents of each chapter.

Chapter 2 offers a literature review on the definitions and the categorizations of opposites in previous studies.

Chapter 3 is for the first study we have on Chinese opposites in constructions from bi-syllable to quad-syllable. The result shows the basic co-occurring patterns of opposite pairings and the function of each pattern. This chapter also explores the ordering rules for opposite pairing members on morphological level.

Chapter 4 is for the second study on Chinese opposites in context-free discourse. We extend the method in study 1 (Chap. 3) to discourse level to observe the distributions of related syntactic frames in complementary, antonym and converse. We also compare the Chinese results with the ones of English and Japanese and generalize the features of Chinese opposites. At the same time, this study answers what canonical opposites are and whether they exist in our data.

Chapter 5 discusses the relation between opposites and negation frames. In study 2 (Chap. 4), we notice that negation frames do not take a high percentage in the syntactic frame distribution. This finding is against our intuition. Hence, we use negation frames to see what semantic relations would be triggered out. The result refreshes our understanding to the relation between negation and opposites, as well as the functions of negation frames have with different semantic relations.

In the Conclusion part (Chap. 6), we summarize the findings of the three studies, answer the two research questions presented in Chap. 1, and point out how this work innovates on the topic of opposites, and what would be expected in our next work.

Chapter 2
Literature Review

2.1 Definition and Categorization

Generally speaking, oppositeness is defined as two words holding contrast meanings (cf. Lyons 1968, 1977; Cruse 1986, 2004; Murphy 2003; Cann 1993, 2002; Steven 2002) and it is agreed by Chinese researchers (cf. Sheng 1958; Fu 1996; Shi 1983; Jiang 2000; Xu 2000; He et al. 2005; Zhang 2009). But any native speaker of Chinese would naturally feel that the way of how 死 *si3/dead* contrasts to 活 *huo2/alive* is not the same as the one of how 买 *mai3/buy* contrasts to 卖 *mai4/sell*. There are sub-types of opposites under the general definition.

Lyons, Cruse and their following researchers agree that for the basic distinction within opposites is whether they are gradable and ungradable. The ungradable opposites are termed as "complementaries" (Lyons, 1968; Cruse 1986), or "binary antonyms" (Cann 2011), while the gradable ones are called "antonyms" (Lyons 1968, 1977; Cruse 1986, 2004). For the rest opposites, Lyons (1968, 1977) defines pairs like *buy: sell*, *husband: wife* as "converses" and pairs like *come: go*, *up: down* as "directional opposites".

Cruse (1986) makes a further distinction among opposites by directions, for example: antipodals are the ones "in which one term represents an extreme in one direction along some salient axis, while the other term denotes the corresponding extreme in the other direction", like *all: none*, *black: white*; and, counterparts, "which essential defining directions are reversed", like *male: female*, *yin: yang*; and, reversives, "those pairs of verbs which denote motion or change in opposite directions", like *rise: fall*, *ascend: descend*; also the relational opposites, that is, converses, are "for the time being at least, by the fact that when one member of a pair is substituted for the other in a sentence the new sentence can be made logically equivalent to the original one by interchanging two of the noun phrase arguments", like *below: above*, *in front of: behind*.

In his later work (Cruse 1994), Cruse modifies the above definitions with prototype theory. That is, for a feature model of prototype structure of certain

J. Ding, *A Lexical Semantic Study of Chinese Opposites*,
Frontiers in Chinese Linguistics 1, https://doi.org/10.1007/978-981-10-6184-4_2

lexical relation, the more some items one pairing manifests, the more central it is in the category.

As to the very common converse pairs, such as *buy: sell*, Croft and Cruse (2004) note that "their oppositeness is not a necessary consequences of their being converses, but arises from other factors (for instance, the oppositeness of the directions of transfer of goods and money in buy and sell)" (cf. 2004: 164–6). For the "dynamic construal approach", the authors mean that, "sense relations are treated as semantic relations… between particular contextual construals of words" (2004: 141), and, "oppositeness is a matter of construal, and it subject to cognitive, conventional and contextual constraints" (2004: 164).

In our studying, we decide to take a rough but clear classification for the overall group of opposites. The word pairs which hold a meaning contrast would be generally called **opposites**. Within that, the ones which are semantically bi-parting the scale/domain, that is, it is supposed to have only two states, A or not A, in a normal or given domain, are called **complementaries**. The typically examples are *dead: alive*, *even: odd*. In other words, the complementary pairs are semantically ungradable. On the other hand, the ones which are semantically gradable are called **antonyms**. Typical examples include: *big: small*, *hot: cold*, *young: old*. The word pairs which are defining the same relation from different aspects, like *husband: wife*, *buy: sell*, are called **converses**. The three sub-types of opposite are the main targets in this paper. Besides, this paper (especially in Chap. 3) also involves cases like *red: black*, *summer: winter*, *happy: sad*, which do not satisfy the definition of either of the three sub-types but are used as contrasting pairs in Chinese. Such pairs are called **taxonomies**. Complementary, antonym and converse are all binary relations while taxonomy is not. Taxonomy relation is a multiple relation (Fig. 2.1).

The advantage of this semantic standard is that, it is unambiguous in practices. That is to say, the category of certain pairing can be entailed from their meanings and there is only one possible relation for a given pair. In saying that, we are referring to the basic or original meaning of the words. In other words, some pragmatic usages of certain pairs, no matter how frequently they behave, cannot be

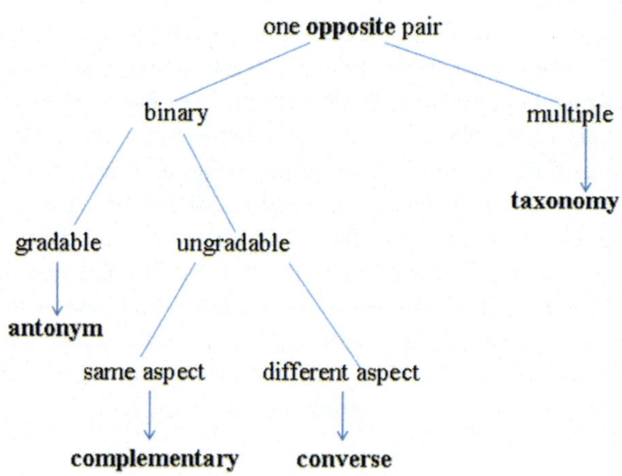

Fig. 2.1 Categorization of opposites

accounted for classifying the related pairs. Hence, the opposite pair of *si3: huo2* is considered as complementary, since the physiological status of normal beings can only be alive or dead. And it would not be changed to antonym even having 半死不活 *ban4/half si3/dead bu4/not huo2/alive* "half dead half alive" is a very commonly used saying in Chinese.

Our definition of opposite overlaps with the main storm studies of opposites (cf. Lyons 1968, 1977; Cruse 1986, 2004; Cann 1993, 2002, 2011; Steven 2002; Murphy 2003). The gradable/ungradable distinguish between antonym and complementary is accepted by most of the researchers (Lyons 1968, 1977; Cruse 1986, 2004; Steven 2002; Murphy 2003; Croft and Cruse 2004; Cann 2011).

We cover "directional opposite" in Lyons (1968, 1977), which is exampled as *up: down,* as well as the "polar antonym", "overlapping antonym", "equipollent antonym" (Cruse 1986; Croft and Cruse 2004), in the category of antonym. The term antonym is equal to the "gradable contrary" in Murphy (2003). For the category of converse, it has a majority agreement among Lyons (1977), Cruse (1986), Cann (1993) and Murphy (2003). We employ the word taxonomy to refer to the multiple contrasting pairs, in response to Mettinger's (1994) "non-systemic semantic opposition", in his three levels of meaning contrasts and pragmatic usages of some non-binary contrast word pairs in natural language, and, similar to Cann's (1993) "opposite" which can shift from "hyponymy".

2.2 Some Properties of Being Opposite

2.2.1 Canonicity

Opposite pairs are assumed to be stored in human mind as conceptual opposite in nature (Murphy 2003; Paradis 2003, 2005; Paradis et al. 2009; Willners and Paradis 2010). That means for the two opposite concepts there could be more than one possible pairing since each concept would have various lexicalized words.

It somehow agrees with the Prototype Theory. The Prototype Theory can be traced back to Wittgenstein's notion of "family resemblance", which is illustrated by the famous GAME example and generate into a theory after Eleanor Rosch's categorizing for internal structures in 1970s (cf. Geeraerts 2002).

For the lexical relation studies, early researchers do not employ the term 'prototype' but also realize the fact that some pairs may be thought as better pairings than the others. Lehrer and Lehrer (1982) firstly distinguish *perfect* antonym pairs, like *hot: cold*, from the imperfect antonym, like *hot: cool*. The criterion is whether they have the same "[similarity] distance from the midinterval" (cf. 1982: 488–90). Herrmann et al.'s (1986) later criteria also include the clarity of the dimensions on which the pairs are based as well as the distances from the midpoint of the domain should be equal for both opposite members.

Cruse's (1994) "prototype effects" of being opposites include: fuzzy boundaries, graded goodness-of-examplar scores; early and frequent mention by subjects to list members of categories; early acquisition; faster verification of category member pairs; stronger priming effect of category name on member. Under such a theory, Cruse re-defines opposites as a general category, which should be diametric, symmetric, binary and exhaustively dividing superordinate domain. Cruse also mentions that these features are not simply present or absent but in some sense gradable.

Croft and Cruse (2004: 166f) summarize the criteria of judging the goodness of an opposite pair: (a) intrinsic binarity ("within the appropriate domain, there are only two possibilities", or "[a]t a more abstract level, there are only two directions of change between two states", which "have a kind of built-in logical twoness", but not self-sufficient in many cases); (b) the "purity" of the opposition (for example, for the basic opposition of MALE: FEMALE, the pair of *male: female* is better in the opposite sense than the one of *man: woman*, while the later one is better than the one of *aunt: uncle*); (c) symmetry (symmetrically disposed about the reference point); (d) matched non-propositional features (non-propositional features should be the same for both members of a pair). (2004: 166–7)

The term "canonicity", sometimes "canonical antonym" or "antonym canonicity", is widely used by recent studies on deciding good (or even "super" good) antonym pairing members. Following the cognitive prototype approach (Cruse 1994, 2004; Croft and Cruse 2004) mentioned above, researchers (for example, Murphy 2003; Jones and Murphy 2005; Paradis et al. 2006, 2009; Jones et al. 2007; Willners and Paradis 2010; Jones et al. 2012) show great interests in using corpora and experiments to measure the canonicity of antonym pairings. These studies mainly focus on English but also some work for other languages like Swedish and Japanese.

To start with, what is "canonicity"? Then, what is "canonical antonym"? Or, what is "antonym canonicity"? And, most importantly and interestingly, how to measure it?

Murphy (2003: 31) defines the canonicity of antonym is "the extent to which antonyms are both semantically related and conventionalized as pairs in language". Paradis et al. (2009) then extends the definition and further explains, "A high degree of canonicity means a high degree of lexico-semantic entrenchment in memory and conventionalization in text and discourse, and a low degree of canonicity means weak or no entrenchment and conventionalization of antonym couplings. The lexical aspect of canonicity concerns *which* words pairs are located *where* on a scale from good to bad antonyms and the semantic part focuses on *why* some pairs might be considered better oppositions than others." (2009: 380–1) In short words, the canonical ones are supposed to have a high co-occurrence in contexts as well as in human brain, hence it can be reflected in many aspects of language.

Jones et al. (2007) uses the World-Wide-Web as corpus to investigate the antonym canonicity from a number of seed words, by building certain lexico-grammatical constructions in discourse, such as *X and Y alike*, *between X and Y*, *both X and Y*, *either X or Y*, *from X to Y*, *X versus Y* and *whether X or Y*, which are identified by Jones (2002).

Basing on the result of Jones et al. (2007) and employing two experiments, one for elicitation and one for judgment, Paradis et al. (2009) then continue the work of defining what good opposites are. They conclude that there is a small but distinct group of conventionalized canonical antonyms, also, a continuum from excellent antonym pairings with a total participant consensus to pairings with a steady decrease in agreement. Antonymy, as their findings, is primarily a conceptual relation in that binary contrast is always a possibility in meaning construals and such construals are based on general knowledge-intensive cognitive processes.

2.2.2 Markedness

Some opposite pairs are said to have one member as unmarked and the other as marked. Several methods can be used to test which one is unmarked. A literature review on it has been done by Ding and Huang (2013) and we cited their work as follow.

Firstly, a common method is the neutralized question (Lehrer 1985; Lyons 1968, 1977).

It is normal to accept a question like:

How long is it?

Rather than:

How short is it?

The first sentence is always considered as a natural way to ask for the length of something, without any presupposition. So the answer to the first question is free from the limitation of length range—it can be thousands and millions of miles, like for the distance from earth to the sun, but also can be only a few millimeters, like for the measurement of a cell.

In contrast, when using the sentence of "How short is it", the speaker is actually having the supposition that the object he or she refers to is supposed to be short, or shorter than the expected length. So if a basketball player falls to be selected into the national team, because of his height, people might ask: "How short is he?" Even the fact is a basketball player is probably higher than the majority of population. So the marked question, could be "*How short is he?*" but not "*How tall is he?*", "carry with the presupposition that the object in question has already been placed towards one end of the scale rather than the other" (Lyons 1968: 467).

The unmarkedness of opposite members is also "neutralized" (Lyons 1968: 467) by that of nominalization. We may already notice that the word "length", which derives from the word "long", is now used as the term for such property. The above question of "How long is it" can also be uttered as "What is the length of it", but not "what is the shortness of it". Similarly, it is "shortness", rather than "length", that selected for the presupposition that the object is in the scale of being short, or shorter than expectation. According to Lyons (1968), the fact of the neutralization is that people may feel one of the opposite pair is "positive" while the other "negative". So for the *long: short* pair, *long* is treated as a more-than-normal size, and short as less-than-normal size. In general, people prefer to neutralize the "more than" one as the 'unmarked' one.

Besides, it is natural to use one of the pair as Quantity Measure Adjective (Lehrer 1985). To the question of "How long is it", we usually answer: "It is 5 feet *long*." But not: "It is 5 feet *short*." Unless in: "It is 5 feet shorter than you want." It is the same situation for ratios: utterances like "A is twice/half as long as B" are preferred than "A is twice/half as short as B".

For a limited number of English opposite pairs, it is much easier to indicate which one is the unmarked. Take *happy: unhappy* for example. The later obviously has a morphological markedness of prefix "un-" in its form. And *happy* may be called as the "base-form" of the pair which is morphologically positive, but the other one, *unhappy,* morphologically negative[1] (Lyons 1977). This criterion may be a little tricky if applied to Chinese, since the definition of prefix, suffix and root in English morphology is very problematic in Chinese. For many lexicalized concepts, it is possible to add a negator 不 *bu4/not* to them, shifting from, such as, 快乐 *kuai4le4/happy* to 不快乐 *bu4/not kuai4lei4/happy*. But for some Chinese lexicographers (Liu and Zhou 1995), the character numbers of an opposite pairing are restricted to be the same, except the ones with syllabic suffix like 儿*er0*. So, words like 伤心 *shang1xin1/sad* can be an opposite pairing to 快乐 *kuai4le4/happy* but phrases like 不快乐 *bu4/not kuai4lei4/happy* cannot.

Lehrer (1985) lists three properties of the unmarked one. The first one is "the unmarked member is evaluatively positive; the marked is negative" (Lehrer 1985: 400). It might be questioned on how the positive or negative is defined. For pairs such as *good: bad*, it is easy. But for pairs like *big: small*, the answer may change with contexts. The second one is "the unmarked member denotes more of a quality"; and the third one is "the unmarked member is less likely to be 'biased' or 'committed'" in "asymmetrical entailments". We may find that, for some opposite pairs, neither of the two properties stays consistent in different contexts. Lehrer also admits he often changes his minds when making judgments for those opposite pairs (1985: 401), which of course places a question mark on the applicability of the criteria.

[1]The morphological relation also makes words like *happy* be paired in both gradable and ungradable opposite pairs, like *happy: angry* and *happy: unhappy*. (Lyons 1977: 275).

Chapter 3
Opposites in Constructions

3.1 Research Question

This chapter is going to see how the opposite pairs are used in constructions from bi-syllabic to quad-syllabic. In other words, how the opposites are used on morphological level.

3.2 Methodology, Candidate List and Corpus

We use the lexicon of Sinica Corpus for the study. Sinica Corpus is one of the largest balanced corpora for Modern Chinese so its lexicon is supposed to contain a wide range of words in Chinese.

There are two main steps in our experiment: first, selecting a candidate list of opposite pairs; then, putting the list into corpus to extract the words containing these opposite pairings.

Xinhua Dictionary of Opposites (《新华反义词词典》 2003) is selected as the base of our candidate list. It is the most authoritative dictionary for Chinese opposites, and its definition of what an opposite pair is, is based on the lexical meanings. That is to say, for the two members of an opposite pair: the assertion of one member implies the negation of the other, and vice versa, like 生:死 (*sheng1/living: si3/death*); or, the meanings of two members are contrasts of each other, but the negation of one does not necessarily imply the assertion of the other, like 大:小 (*da4/big: xiao3/small*); or, converse pairs like 买:卖 (*mai3/buy: mai4/sell*). In that way, it covers most of the common opposite pairs in Chinese. However, the book does not include pairs like 夫:妻 (*fu1/husband: qi1/wife*), which are also very frequently used as opposites in Chinese. For this, we added an extra 39 pairs to the initial list; hence, the final seed list contains 295 pairs, which are

J. Ding, *A Lexical Semantic Study of Chinese Opposites*,
Frontiers in Chinese Linguistics 1, https://doi.org/10.1007/978-981-10-6184-4_3

supposed to cover the most commonly used opposites Chinese. A full list of the seed pairings can be found in Appendix A.

In this study, an opposite pairing is generalized as [A] and [−A]. [A] and [−A] are decided by the order they have in constructions. If there are two pairings in the same construction, the first pairing will be [A1] and [−A1], the second one will be [A2] and [−A2].

The synonyms are marked as [S] and [S′], according to their sequences in the construction.

Some words in the construction are not opposite or synonym pairings and they will be marked as [X], or [X1] [X2] and so on, if necessary. Sometimes, a linking word is separated into two parts, then the first part will be marked as [X−] and the second part as [+X].

3.3 Result

The result shows that there are four basic patterns in our data. The first pattern only contains one opposite pairing, which is generalized as [A][−A], such as in 美丑 *mei3/beauty chou3/ugliness* “appearance”, 胜负 *sheng4/victory fu4/failure* “result of the competition”, 爱恨 *ai4/love hen4/hate* “emotions”, 男女 *nan2/man nv3/woman* “man and woman”. This basic pattern [A][−A] sometimes forms into patterns of [A][−A][A][−A], [A][A][−A][−A] and [A][−A][A].

The second one is that of one opposite pairing with one relational word or linking word. The relation or a linking word may appear in front/behind the pairing, like [A][−A][X] 买卖婚姻 *mai3/buy mai4/sell hun1yin1/marriage* “marriage by purchase” or [X][A][−A] 举国上下 *ju3guo2/all_nation_wide shang4/up xia4/down* “the whole nation”; or, in the middle position of the pattern, like [A][X][−A] 老来少 *lao3/old lai2/become shao3/young* “an old man with a young heart”; or, be separated into two parts interjecting the two opposite members, like [X−][A][+X][−A] 自上而下 *zi4/from shang4/up er2/to xia4/down* “from up to down” and [A][X−][−A][+X] 古为今用 *gu3/ancient wei2/for jin1/modern yong4/use* “learning from the past”.

The third pattern is combined by two opposite pairings. For example, [A1][A2][−A1][−A2], 古往今来 *gu3/ancient wang3/go jin1/nowadays lai2/come* “all the times”, and, [A1][−A1][A2][−A2], 男女老少 *nan2/man nv3/woman lao3/old shao4/young* “all the peoples”.

The forth one is a combination of one opposite pairing and one synonym pairing, like 东躲西藏 *dong1/east duo3/shun xi1/west cang2/hide* “hide oneself (from place to place)” is marked as [A][S][−A][S′]. And, in some of the cases, the added word repeats in the same patterns, such as 时冷时热 *shi2/sometimes leng3/cold shi2/sometimes re4/hot* “sometimes cold and sometimes hot”, which is marked as [S][A][S][−A] (Table 3.1).

Table 3.1 Hits of four basic patterns and their variations

Category	Pattern	Hits	Total
One opposite pairing	[A][−A]	218	
	[A][A][−A][−A]	38	
	[A][−A][A][−A]	3	
	[A][−A][A]	1	
			260
One opposite pairing with linking word(s)	[A][−A][X]	459	
	[X][A][−A]	120	
	[X−][A][+X][−A]	63	
	[A][X][−A]	62	
	[A][X−][−A][+X]	6	
			710
Two opposite pairings	[A1][A2][−A1][−A2]	115	
	[A1][−A1][A2][−A2]	21	
			136
One opposite pairing with one synonym pairing	[S][A][S][−A]	216	
	[A][S][−A][S′]	129	
	[S][A][S′][−A]	118	
	[A][S][−A][S]	17	
			480
1586			

3.3.1 [A][−A] and Its Derived Patterns

This construction is the base of all the others. In the 218 examples, there are combinations of complementary pairings, like 生死 *sheng1/life si3/death* “life-and-death”, 男女 *nan2/man nv3/woman* “man and woman”, 开合 *kai1/open he2/closed* “open and closed”; and that of antonym pairings, like 松紧 *song1/loose jin3/tight* “tightness”, 安危 *an1/safe wei1/danger* “safety”, 长短 *chang1/long duan3/short* “length”; and that of converse pairings, like 夫妻 *fu1/husband qi1/wife* “a couple”, 购销 *gou4/buy xiao1/sell* “buy and sell”, 嫁娶 *jia4/marriage (from women’s aspect) qv3/marriage (from men’s aspect)* “marriage”. Taxonomy is also possible to generate [A][−A] constructions; for example, 红白 *hong2/red bai2/white* “red and white”, 文武 *wen2/civil wu3/military* “civil and military”, 水火 *shui3/water huo3/fire* “water and fire”. They are considered as contrasting pairs in Chinese culture.

The words in [A][−A] constructions are often lexicalized. For example, 东西 *dong1/east xi1/west* "issue":

(1) 吃点东西吧!

chi1/eat dian3/some dong1/east xi1/west ba0/BA!
"Let's eat something!"

In the sense of "issue", *dong1xi1* is the only accepted order of *dong1* and *xi1*; the reversed form of * 西东 *xi1dong1* is not accepted. But in the sense of direction, sometimes *xi1dong1* is also acceptable:

(2) 各奔东西

ge4/each ben1/run_to dong1/east xi1/west
* 各奔西东
ge4/each ben1/run_to xi1/west dong1/east
"separate in different places"

For some of the combinations, their meanings change according to the various contexts, although the basic meanings stay unchanged. For example, the combination of 早 *zao3/morning* and 晚 *wan3/evening*:

(3) 早晚温差大

zao3/morning wan3/evening wen1/temperature cha1/difference da4/big
"the differences in temperature between morning and evening is great"

(4) 新闻早晚报

xin1wen2/news zao3/morning wan3/night bao4/report
"an updated news message in the morning and in the evening (everyday)"

(5) 早晚要发达

zao3/morning wan3/evening yao4/will fa1da2/rich
"to be rich sooner or later"

In sentence (a) and (b), *zao3wan3* refers to the literal interpretation of morning and evening, and in (a) it is used to modify the noun *wen1cha1* "differences of temperature", in (b) it is modifying the verb *bao4* "to report". In sentence (c) *zao3wan3* means "sooner or later", and is used as an adverb of the phrase *yao4fa1da2* "to be rich".

Another example is 左右 *zuo3/left you4/right*: which bears the basic meaning in such sentences like:

(6) 伴随在我左右

ban4sui2/accompany zai4/PREP wo3/I zuo3/left you4/right
"to accompany me"

(7) 左右事件的发展

zuo3/left you4/right shi4jian4/event de0/DE fa1zhan3/development
"to make great influence on the development of the event"

The basic meaning of *zuo3you4* is "the nearby place of (something or someone)", as in sentence (a). In sentence (b), *zuo3you4* is used as a verb, which can be understood as "to make the event develop to any direction (to right or to left) as someone wants". For that meaning, *zuo3you4* is the only compound that is combined by the directional words. That is to say, neither of the other compounds of directional words, such as *dong1xi1*, *nan2bei3*, *shang4xia4* and so on, has developed the similar meaning like *zuo3you4*.

Sometimes, both orders are acceptable, but the meanings are different. For example, 反正 *fan3/back zheng4/front* means "anyway" while 正反 *zheng4/front fan3/back* means "both (sides)" so *fan3zheng4* and *zheng4fan3*are not exchangeable in contexts:

(8) 反正要考试的,不如平时好好学习.

fan3/back zheng4/front yao4/need kao3shi4/examine de0/DE, bu4ru2/it_would_be_better_to ping1shi2/in_normal_times hao3/good hao3/good xue2xi2/study
"Since examination is unavoidable, we should stay hard in the semester."

(9) 正反两面

zheng4/front fan3/back liang3/two mian4/CL
* 反正两面

fan3/back zheng4/frontliang3/two mian4/CL.
"both sides"

Such compounds and their ordering are discussed in Sect. 3.4.2.

When [A][−A] pattern is derived into the [A][A][−A][−A] pattern, the meaning of the [A][A][−A][−A] compound is similar to the original meaning of [A][−A] compound. For many of the opposite pairings, the combinations of [A][−A] and [A][−A][A][−A] do not show obvious differences in contextual usage. Let's take 上下 *shang4/up xia4/down* and 上上下下 *shang4/up shang4/up xia4/down xia4/down* "up and down" for example:

(10) 我<u>上下</u>打量了他一番.

wo3/Ishang4/up shang4/up xia4/down xia4/down da3liang4/look le0/LE ta1/he yi1/one fan1/CL
我<u>上上下下</u>打量了他一番.
wo3/Ishang4/up shang4/up xia4/down xia4/down da3liang4/look le0/LE ta1/he yi1/one fan1/CL
"I looked him up and down."

In some cases, *shang4xia4* may be more acceptable than *shang4shang4xia4xia4*:

(11) 上下一条心

shang4/up xia4/down yi1/one tiao2/CL xin1/heart
? 上上下下一条心
shang4/up xia4/down shang4/up xia4/down yi1/one tiao2/CL xin1/heart
"all the people of one mind"

(12) 上下五千年

shang4/up xia4/down wu3/five qian1/thousand nian2/year
? 上上下下五千年
shang4/up shang4/up xia4/down xia4/down
"all the five thousand years"

And in other cases, *shang4shang4xia4xia4* is better than *shang4xia4*:

(13) ? 现在公司上下都知道他被解雇了.

xian4zai4/now gong1si1/company shang4/up xia4/down dou1/all zhi1dao4/know ta1/he bei4/BEI jie3gu4/fire le0/LE
现在公司上上下下都知道他被解雇了.
xian4zai4/now gong1si1/company shang4/up shang4/up xia4/down xia4/down dou1/all zhi1dao4/know ta1/he bei4/BEI jie3gu4/fire le0/LE
"Now all the people in the company know that he is fired."

(14) ? 警察把这座房子上下都搜遍了.

jing3cha2/policeman ba3/BA zhe4/this zuo4/CL fang2zi0/house shang4/up xia4/down dou1/all sou1/search bian4/all le0/LE
警察把这座房子上上下下都搜遍了.
jing3cha2/policeman ba3/BA zhe4/this zuo4/CL fang2zi0/house shang4/up shang4/up xia4/down xia4/down dou1/all sou1/search bian4/all le0/LE
"The policeman searched the house from cellar to rafter."

In these cases, *shang4shang4xia4xia4* is used to emphasize the meaning of "all the parts/things/people/…".

In these above sentences, both *shang4xia4 and shang4shang4xia4xia4* can be acceptable and replaceable to each other. But in some other cases, only *shang4xia4* can be used, not *shang4shang4xia4xia4*:

(15) 三十岁上下

san1shi2/thirty sui4/CLshang4/up xia4/down
* 三十岁上上下下
san1shi2/thirty sui4/CLshang4/up shang4/up xia4/down xia4/down
"around thirty-year old"

In these cases, *shang4xia4* means “around”, not “ups and downs”. It is similar to that of 左右 *zuo3/left you4/right*, “around”:

(16) 三十岁左右

san1shi2/thirty sui4/CLzuo3/left you4/right
* 三十岁左左右右
san1shi2/thirty sui4/CLzuo3/left zuo3/left you4/right you4/right
“around thirty-year old”

The word *zuo3zuo3you4you4* is actually not accepted for native speakers.

In other cases, the compounds of [A][−A] pattern and [A][A][−A][−A] pattern with the same opposite pairing do not have the same meaning and therefore their usages are different. For example, *lai2wang3* can be used to modify the nouns and also as a verb, while for *lai2lai2wang3wang3*, the latter usage is not allowed:

(17) 来来往往

lai1/come lai1/come wang3/leave wang3/leave
“the coming and going (people)”

(18) 我喜欢看来来往往的行人.

wo3/I xi3huan1/like kan4/seelai1/come lai1/come wang3/leave wang3/leave de0/DE xing2ren2/pedestrian
“I like to watch people going by.”

Lai2lai2wang3wang3 is allowed to modify *xing2ren2*, “pedestrian”, as *lai2-wang3* does to *che1liang4*, “vehicle”. Meanwhile, as 和某人来往 (“being friends with someone”) is common, but * 和某人来来往往 does not sound natural to Chinese speakers.

For complementary pairings like 男 *nan2/man* 女 *nv3/woman*, the compound of *nan2nv3* refers to the general human being, like:

(19) 饮食男女

yin3/drink shi2/eat nan2/man nv3/woman
“common people with common issues.”

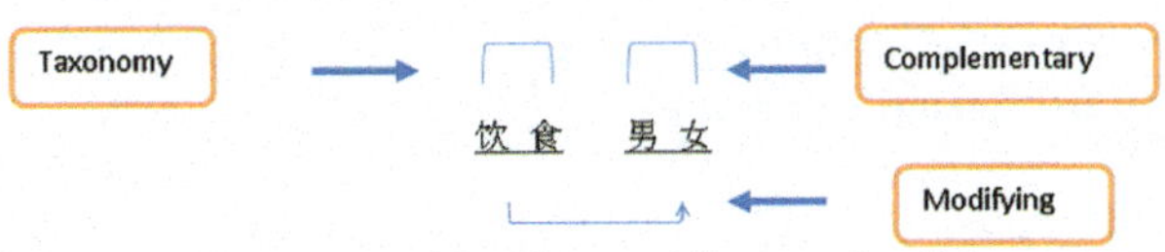

Yin3shi2 is one combination, while *nan2nv3* is another one. *Yin3* and *shi2* are two common kinds of daily activities and are often used as the hyponyms of the latter. Hence this compound refers to all the daily activities, and serves to modify the other compound *nan2nv3*. *Nan3* and *nv3* may separate in some compounds:

(20) 红男绿女

hong2/red nan2/man lv4/green nv3/woman
“colorful dressed men and women”

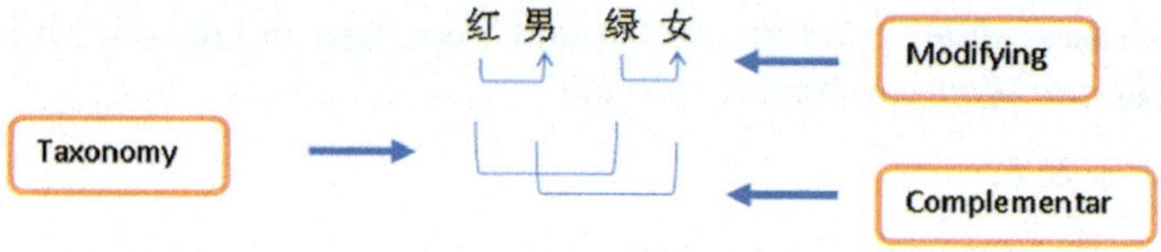

Nan2 and *nv3*comprise one pair of opposites. Apparently, *hong2* and *lv4* are two taxonomies of color terms. *Hong2* modifies *nan2* and *lv4* modifies *nv3*. Actually it is one special figure of speech in Chinese, called 互文 *hu4wen2*, which means the two parts (sometimes more than two parts) are supplementary of and dependent on each other. Therefore, the *hong2* is also indirectly modifying *nv3*, and the same applies to *lv4* for *nan2*. The phrase can be understood as 红绿 *hong2lv4* + 男女 *nan2nv3*, as the same construction of 饮食男女 *yin3shi2 nan2nv3*, where *hong2lv3* refers to the numerous kinds of colors, and *nan2nv3* to general human beings. And, when the pattern is doubled, the meaning of the derived one is the same:

(21) 男男女女

nan2/man nan2/man nv3/woman nv3/woman
'men and women'
我使自己活在另一个世界里,看见那里的<u>男男女女</u>怎样欢笑、哭泣. (巴金《秋》)
wo3/I shi3/make zi4ji3/oneself huo2/live zai4/at ling4yi1ge4/another shi4jie4/world, kan4jian4/see na4li3/there de0/DE nan2/man nan2/man nv3/woman nv3/woman zen3yang4/how huan1xiao4/laugh, ku1qi4/cry
"I make myself living in another world to see the people there experiencing their lifes."

In most cases, it is safe to say that all the pairings which can combine the patterns of [A][A][−A][−A], can also be reduced into the form of [A][−A], and still keep the same function of referring to the whole scale. But the reverse does not apply. Firstly, not all the compounds of [A][−A] can grow into the form of [A][A][−A][−A], for example, 夫妻 *fu1/husband qi1/wife* "husband and wife":

(22) 柴米<u>夫妻</u>

chai2/fire_wood mi3/ricefu1/husband qi1/wife
"a couple who live from hand to mouth"

(23) * 夫夫妻妻

fu1/husband fu1/husband qi1/wife qi1/wife
"all the husband and wife"

Reversely, some opposite pairings can occur in the form of [A][A][−A][−A], but are not lexicalized when used as [A][−A]:

(24) 吞吞吐吐

tun1/swallow tu3/spit tun1/swallow tu3/spit
"(to speak) humming and hawing"
他说话吞吞吐吐,一点儿都不爽快!
ta1/he shuo1hua4/speak tun1/swallow tu3/spit tun1/swallow tu3/spit de0/DE, yi1/one dian3er0/CL dou1/all bu4/not shuang1kuai4/straight
"He speaks humming and hawing, not frank at all!"

(25) *吞吐[1]

tun1/swallow tu3/spit
"(usually for port) to take in and to send out"
*该港口去年吞吐了三千万吨货物.
gai1/this gang3kou3/port qu4nian2/last_year tun1/swallow tu3/spit le0/LE san3/three qian1wang4/ten_million dun1/ton huo4/wu4/goods
"Last year, there was thirty million tons of goods going through this port."

But the combination of *tun1* and *tu3* is also lexicalized in the form of [A][−A][X]:

(26) 吞吐量

tun1/swallow tu3/spit liang4/quantity
"throughput"
该港口去年的吞吐量有三千万吨.
gai1/this gang3kou3/port qu4nian2/last_year de0/DE tun1/swallow tu3/spit liang4/quantity you3/have qian1wang4/ten_million dun1/ton
"The throughput of this port in last year was thirty million tons."

There are also some cases in which the meaning of the combination might be different when used as [A][−A] and as [A][A][−A][−A]:

(27) 开关

kai1/open guan1/close
"switch"
电灯开关
dian4deng1/electric_light kai1/open guan1/close
"light switch"

[1]The examples here are for Modern Chinese. 吞吐 in ancient Chinese can also be used as a verb, for example, 吞吐百川 *tun1/swallow tu3/spit bai3/hundred chuan1/river* "to take and spit hundreds of rivers" (*Bao Zhao*, Southern Dynasty, "Deng Dalei An YU Mei Shu"), or as a noun 吞吐之术 *tun1/swallow tu3/spit zhi1/ZHI shu4/method* "(for Taoism) regulating respiration", or used as 吞吞吐吐, like in 言词吞吐 *yan2/speak ci2/wordtun1/swallow tu3/spit* "to speak humming and hawing" (*Mao Jing*, Ming Dynasty, "Jiao Pa Ji").

(28) 开开关关

kai1/open kai1/open guan1/close guan1/close
"repeating turn on and off"
电灯开开关关更耗电.
dian4deng1/electric_light kai1/open kai1/open guan1/close guan1/close geng4/more hao4/use dian4/power
"Repeating turn on and off the light is more power consumptive."

[A][−A][A][−A], [A][−A][A] and [A][−A][−A][A] patterns are also possible in daily discourse, but the prevalence of these groupings is much lower than the other kinds. Examples of [A][−A][A][−A] include:

(29) 彼此彼此 *bi3/there ci3/here bi3/there ci3/here* "same here"

——您辛苦了
nin2/you xin1ku3/tired le0/LE
"Thanks for your hard work!"
——彼此彼此.
bi3/there ci3/here bi3/there ci3/here
"Same here."

And for pattern of [A][−A][A], such as 里外里[2] *li3/inside wai4/outside li3/inside* "totally"

(30) 咱们亲兄弟,钱放在谁口袋,里外里是一样的.

zan1men0/we qin1xiong1di4/blood_brother, qian2/money fang4/put zai4/at shui2/who kou3dai4/pocket, li3/inside wai4/outside li3/inside shi4/be yi1yang4/the_same de0/DE
"We are blood brothers, so it is no difference for whom to take the money."

聚散离合 *ju4/gather san4/depart li2/depart he1/gather* "to gather and to depart" is a very special case in its combination of two opposite pairings:

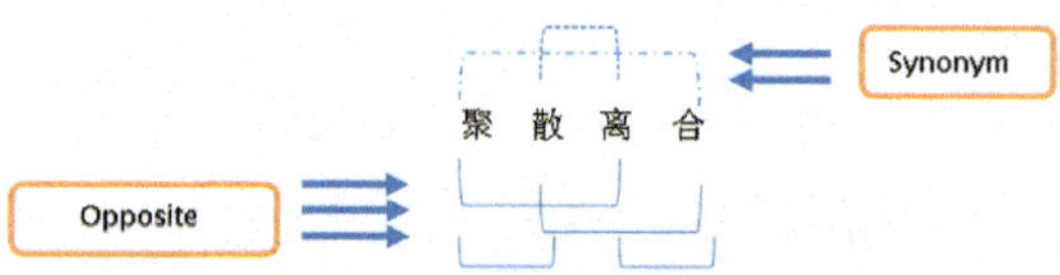

Sentences with *ju4san4li2he1* like:

[2]In Taiwanese Chinese, it is more common to say 里外里面*li3/inside wai4/outside li3mian4/inside* "totally".

(31) 人世间聚散离合是很正常的事情.

renshi4jian1/in_the_worldju4/gather san4/depart li2/depart he1/gather shi4/be hen3/very zheng4chang2/common de0/DE shi4qing2/thing
"It is very common to experience gathering and departing in the human world."

3.3.2 [A][−A][X] and Its Derived Patterns

The second basic pattern is that of one opposite pairing with some relation represented in the same pattern. Since the semantic relation between the pair members may vary, the sub-categories of this pattern are also very rich. Within the known patterns of this category, [A][−A][X] is the most common, and may also be the most productive one in usage. Therefore, it is chosen as the representative pattern of this group.

In the [A][−A][X] pattern, the root for representing the semantic relation is placed in the end of the pattern, marked as [X]. Sometimes, [X] is realized by a nominal root, like 起落架 *qi3/up luo4/down jia4/frame* "undercarriage", or, 买卖婚姻 *mai3/buy mai4/sell hun1/marriage yin1/marriage* "marriage for purchase", and at others, by a verbal root, like 众寡悬殊 *zhong4/many gua3/few xuan2/suspending shu1/different* "a great gap in numerical strength"; 本末倒置 *ben3/root mo4/end dao4/reverse zhi4/place* "treat the incidental more important than the fundamental".

Within this sub-pattern, the compounds such as 南北极 *nan2/south bei3/north ji2/pole* "south and north poles", are also known as **telescope compounds**, since they are formed by extracting the first morpheme of the two compounds (e.g. *nan2* and *bei3*) and their overlapping root (e.g. *-ji2*). In other words, *nan2bei3ji2* is the blend of *nan2ji2* "south pole" and *bei3ji2* "north pole".

起落架 *qi3/up luo4/down jia4/frame* "undercarriage", on the other hand, represents a different case. Although the actions of (rising) up and (falling) down may be done respectively, there is no **qi3jia4* "up carriage" or **luo4jia4* "down carriage" in Chinese. *Qi3luo4* together refers to the action of an under carriage, therefore *qi3luo4jia4* is not a blend of two independent compounds.

The Chinese translation of *The Count of Monte-Christo*[3] is 基督山恩仇记 *ji1du1shan1/Monte_Christo en1/love chou2/hate ji4/story*. The story itself does not only hang on the emotion of love or revenge but covers a rather more complicated relationship. *En1/love* and *chou2/hate* here are supposed to refer to the mixed and dim emotions inspired by the story, and they are paired because they are the most strongly contrasted ones. Hence, the compound of *en1chou2* implies the

[3]*Le Comte de Monte-Cristo, by Alexandire Dumas, 1844.*

"emotions". Similar cases include: 书剑恩仇录[4] *shu1/book jian4/sworden1/love chou2/hatelu4/story*, 一笑泯恩仇 *yi1/one xiao4/smile min3/diminish en1/love chou2/hate* "laugh away", 个人恩怨 *ge4ren2/personalen1/love yuan4/hate* "personal emotions" and so on.

However, the taxonomy of aging words is closer to the situation of *nan2bei3ji2*, rather than that of emotions. In Chinese, the most common used words for ages are:

幼	少	青	中	老
you4/infancy	*shao4/juvenile*	*qing1/youngster*	*zhong1/middle age*	*lao3/elder*

There are sayings like:

(32) 青少年合唱团

qing1/youngster shao4/juvenile nian2/year he2chang4tuan2/chorus
"youth chorus"

(33) 中青年技术骨干

zhong1/middle-aged qing1/youngster nian2/year ji4shu4/technical gu3gan4/backbone
"key technicians who are between young and middle ages"

(34) 中老年奶粉

zhong1/middle-aged lao3/elder nian2/year nian3fen3/milk-power
"milk power for middle-aged and elder people"

We can see these words are blends of *qing1nian2* and *shao4nian2*, *zhong1nian2* and *qing1nian2*, *zhong1nian2* and *lao3nian2*, respectively. The combination of continuous aging words might be more than only two:

(35) 老中青三代艺术家同台献艺

lao3/elder zhong1/middle-aged qing1/youngster san1/three dai4/CL yi4shu4jia1/artists tong2/same tai2/stage xian4yi4/perform
"artists from young to old ages to perform on the same stage"

However, *you4* and *shao4* are rarely be used together. Hence, the combination of two continuous aging words is highly accepted, except for the one of *you4* and *shao4*.

On the other hand, the combinations of non-neighboring words, such as *qing1* and *lao3*, or *zhong1* and *shao4*, or *zhong1* and *you4*, are much less accepted. The

---

[4]Jinyong 1955 (2002), translated by Graham Earnshaw, *The Book & The Sword*, Oxford Publisher, 2005.

only exceptions are the ones of *lao3* and *you4*, or *shao4*. For example, 老少皆宜 *lao3/elder shao4/juvenile jie1/all yi2/suitable*, "be suitable to all the people". The word *zhang3* "(relatively) elder" is also used with *you4* in compounds, as in长幼有序 *zhang3/(relatively)_elder you4/infancy you3/have xu4/order* "the proper order among elders and youngsters".

In other patterns, it is also possible to have the co-occurrence of *lao3* and *you4*, such as: 携老扶幼 *xie2/hold lao3/elder fu2/assist you4/infancy* "to assist the old and the young", 尊老爱幼 *zun1/respect lao3/elder ai4/protect you4/infancy* "to respect the old and protect the young", which both follow the [S][A][S][−A] pattern. And we have the term 老来少 *lao3/elder lai2/come shao4/young*, to describe the people who are at an old age but still full of energy in body and/or mind, which would be classified as [A][X][−A] pattern.

As to the [X][A][−A] pattern, the relation appears in front of the opposite pair, like 争高低 *zheng1/compete_for gao1/up di1/down* "to compete to see which one is better", 跑买卖 *pao3/run mai3/buy mai4/sell* "be on a business travel", or, like 浑身上下 *hun2/all shen1/body shang4/up xia4/down* "all over the body", 结发夫妻 *jie2/bind fa4/hair fu1/husband qi1/wife* "husband and wife of the first marriage".

Shang4xia4 means "all (of _)" and to complete the meaning is to see the part in the preceding position. That is to say, 举国上下 *ju3/all guo2/country shang4/up xia4/down*, means "all the country"; 全家上下 *quan2/all jia1/family shang4/up xia4/down*, means "all the family". The hit number of [A][−A][X] is far more than that of [X][A][−A]. In total, 459 examples are found in the corpus to have the former pattern, while the later one only has 120 hits.

In some other cases, the relation is represented in the position between the pairing members, like [A][X][−A], like 老来少 *lao3/elder lai2/come shao4/young* "an old man with a young heart", 明转暗 *ming2/bright zhuan3/change an4/dark* "turning from bright to dark", 今胜昔 *jin1/today sheng4/win xi1/*past "now is better than the past", and, 供大于求 *gong4/supply da4/big yu2/PREP qiu2/need* "over-supply", 日以继夜[5] *ri4/day yi3/for ji4/continue ye4/night* "around the clock". This sub-pattern is a relatively small one, with only 62 examples found in the corpus.

And the opposite pairings in this sub-pattern are emphasizing the contrasting of the two extreme points. This function is agreed throughout the four major categories. 老来少 *lao3lai2shao4* is the example of an antonym and 供大于求 *gong4da4yu2qiu2* is that of a converse. Additionally, examples of complementary include 生不如死 *sheng1/alive bu4ru2/be_inferior_to si3/dead* "to be dead is better than to be alive", and that of taxonomy are 苦中作乐 *ku3/sorrow zhong1/inside zuo4/make le4/happy* "to seek happiness in sorrow life" and 乐极生悲 *le4/happy ji2/at_most sheng1/give_birth_to bei1/miserable* "misery succeeds happiness".

And for the [A][X][−A] pattern, the four-syllabic structure, which has 59 hits, is obviously more preferred than triple-syllabic structure, which only has 3 hits.

---

[5]It is also common to say 夜以继日 *ye4/nigh yi3/for ji4/continue ri4/day*, and the usage and meaning of the two are actually the same.

Moreover, there are some instances like 量入为出 *liang4/measure ru4/come_in wei4/for chu1/come_out* "to live within one's means", in which the part representing relation breaks into two parts, as *liang4* and *wei2*. Here this pattern is termed as [X−][A][+X][−A].

At the same time, there are also some examples like 外为中用 *wai4/abroad wei2/for zhong1/China yong4/use* "to develop China by using the experience and technics from abroad", and, 恩将仇报 *en1/kindness jiang1/use chou2/ingratitude bao4/repay* "to repay kindness with ingratitude" which will be marked as [A][X−][−A][+X].

There are some fixed frames for both sub-patterns. With the [X−][A][+X][−A] pattern, it is common to have frames like [从][A][到][−A], [自][A][而][−A] or [由][A][及][−A]: 从头到尾 *cong2/from tou2/head dao4/to wei3/*tail "from beginning to the end", 由表及里 *you2/from biao3/surface ji2/to li3/inside* "from outside to inside", 自上而下 *zi4/from shang1/top er2/and xia4/*bottom "all around; from up to bottom". These frames cover all the members of the opposite scale, no matter which category the pairing within them is from. Another popular frame is [化][A][为][−A]: 化整为零 *hua4/change zheng3/whole wei2/as ling2/part* "to break up the whole into parts", 化繁为简 *hua4/change fan2/complex wei2/as jian3/simple* "to simplify something".

And, other common frames include:

[因][A][得][−A]: 因祸得福 *yin1/because huo4/misfortune de2/get fu2/fortune* "to have a blessing in disguise";
[似][A][而][−A]: 似是而非 *si4/like shi4/right er2/but fei1/wrong* "be apparently right but actually wrong";
[以][A][verb][−A] or [借][A][verb][−A]: 以静制动 *yi3/use jing4/steady zhi4/control dong4/dynamic* "to control the dynamic things by steady ones", 借古讽今 *jie4/borrow gu3/ancient feng3/judge jin1/*now "showing one's opinion on present by making comments on the past";
[verb][A][如][−A], [verb][A][若][−A] or [verb][A][成][−A]: 整旧如新 *zheng3/make jiu4/old ru2/as xin1/*new "to repair the old thing until it as a new one", 举重若轻 *ju3/lift zhong4/weighty ruo4/as qing1/weightless* "it seems to have something done easily but actually the work is difficult to deal with", 习非成是 *xi2/accustomed fei1/wrong cheng2/be shi4/right* "accept what is wrong as right when one gets used to it".
As to the [X−][A][+X][−A] pattern, [A][为][−A][用] is relatively common: 外为中用 *wai4wei2zhong1yong4* "to learn from others to develop oneself", and 古为今用 *gu3/ancient wei2/for jin1/today yong4/use* "to learn from history for nowadays' development".

In the corpus, the number of examples of [A][X−][−A][+X] pattern (63 hits) is far greater than that of [X−][A][+X][−A] (6 hits).

3.3.3 [A1][−A1] and [A2][−A2]

This section is for the patterns, which have two opposite pairings. There are two kinds of situations for the pattern. In the first case, the two opposite pairings interrupt with each other, marked as [A1][A2][−A1][−A2]; while in the second, the second pairing members together follow the first one, and is marked as [A1][−A1] [A2][−A2].

The [A1][A2][−A1][−A2] case is represented by 凶多吉少 *xiong1/danger duo1/more ji2/goodness shao3/less* "more dangers than goodness". In this pattern, one of the pairings is used to modify the other. As in *xiong1duo1ji2shao3*, *duo1* is modifying *xiong1* and shao3 is modifying *ji2*, N.A.N.A.[6]

In other cases, it would be possible to have the structures like:

A.N.A.N. 阳儒阴法 *yang2/surfacely ru2/Confucianism yin1/actually fa3/*legalism "to take legalism in the name of Confucianism"
N.V.N.V. 优胜劣汰 *you1/good sheng4/win_out lie4/bad tai4/die_out* "to select out the best and eliminate the others"
V.N.V.N. 贪生怕死 *tan1/seek sheng1/alive pa4/be_afraid_of si3/dead* "be afraid of death and struggle to be alive"
A.V.A.V. 早出晚归 *zao3/early chu1/leave wan3/lately gui1/return* "to leave at a very early time and return when it is very late"
V.A.V.A. 知易行难 *zhi1/know yi4/easy xing2/act nan2/difficult* "it is harder to practice (some rules) than to know (the rules)".

[A1][−A1][A2][−A2] case is represented by *shi4fei1hei1bai2*. So there are two scales in the same pattern:

是-------------非

shi4/right------------fei1/wrong

黑--------------白

hei1/black------------bai2/white

In Chinese culture, *hei1* ("black") is used to refer to being wrong or a criminal (as *fei1*), while *bai2* ("white") to that of right or goodness (as *shi4*). In such a case, there is an overlapping meaning between the two pairings. Hence, the two scales are not the same but semantically related or similar in usage. It can also be proved by the fact that such compounds may also be reduced to bi-syllabic compounds, without meaning changed, via keeping one of the pairing. For example, 颠倒是非黑白 *dian1dao3/confuse shi4fei1hei1bai2/right_and_wrong* is equal to 颠倒是非 *dian1dao3 shi4fei1* or 颠倒黑白 *dian1dao3 hei1bai2*. The use of two scales, we may say, is to double the overlapped meaning of the two pairings.

[6]There are numerous works on Chinese word classes. In order to be consistent, our studying adopts the one used by Sinica Corpus (CKIP 1993; Huang et al. 2008). In which, 'A.' refers to 'Non-predicativeadjective' (非谓形容词), 'N.' refers to noun (体词), 'V.' refers to verb (述词).

No matter what the cases are, the function of this pattern is almost always to cover the whole field of the referred domain, like, 是非黑白 *shi4/right fei1/wrong hei1/black bai2/white* "rights and wrongs" or 安危祸福 *an1/safty wei1/danger huo4/misfortune fu2/fortune* "fortunes and misfortunes".

旦夕祸福, *dan4/day xi1/night huo4/misfortune fu2/fortune*, is one of the few cases which are not used to cover the whole domain. This compound means, fate is unpredictable, and fortune (*fu2*) and misfortune (*huo4*) succeed and change in short time (*dan4xi1*).

That would be explained by the meaning of the compounds. As we can see, the examples above (except *dan4xi1huo4fu2*) are repeating the same/similar/close-related meaning(s) within the same pattern. That is to say, 成败 *cheng2/win bai4/lose* = 得失 *de2/gain shi1/lose*, 生死 *sheng1/alive si3/dead* = 存亡 *cun2/existence wang2/eliminate*; 男女 *nan2/male nv3/female* and 老幼 *lao3/elderly you4/young* both about people, 东西 *dong1/east xi1/west* and 南北 *nan2/south bei3/north* both about directions; 古今 *gu3/ancient jin1/modern* and 中外 *zhong1/China wai4/abroad*, one for historical axis and one for geometric alien, which are both two concepts in Chinese used for referring to the surrounding of human beings, like 上下左右 *shang4/up xia4/down zuo3/right you4/left*, or 宇宙[7] *yu4zhou4/universe*. In other words, they are dependent in some kind of level. But for *dan4xi1huo4fu2*, *dan4xi1* is referring to time while *huo4fu2*, to fate, which are two un-naturally and un-pragmatically related concepts. Hence, *dan4xi1huo4fu2* may be considered more like a phrase, rather than a compound, and therefore develops a different reading method, from the other examples.

3.3.4 [A][−A] and Synonym Pairings

It is necessary to point out that we use the term "synonym" here in a very general manner. It includes the pairings which are usually treated as the ones referring to the same/similar concepts, like 挑 *tian1/select* and 拣 *jian3/pick*, as well as the ones referring to relative (but not the same) concepts, like 街 *jie1/street* and 巷 *xiang4/lane* in 街头巷尾 *jie1/street tou2/head xiang4/lane wei3/tail* "in all the places", 邻 *lin2/neighbor* and 舍 *she4/house* in 左邻右舍 *zuo3/right lin2/neighbor you4/left she4/house* "neighborhood", 腔 *qiang1/accent* and 调 *diao4/tone* in 南腔北调 *nan2/south qiang1/accent bei3/north diao4/tone* "different accents from different places". Pairings like *jie1*: *xiang4*, *lin2*: *she4* and *qiang1*: *diao4* are not synonyms in restricted definition, but are used as synonyms in the compounds. Therefore they are called synonym pairings in this study.

In the four positions ([1][2][3][4]) of a pattern, the one we are going to talk about has two kinds of structures: first, [1] and [3] are a synonym pairing while [2] and [4] are an opposite pairing; and, second, [1] and [3] are an opposite pairing while [2]

[7]Refer to *Wenzi* (《文子》), *Shizi* (《尸子》), *Sancang* (《三苍》), among others.

and [4] are a synonym pairing. The ones like 征战南北 *zheng1/conquer zhan4/fight nan2/south bei3/north* "to fight up and down the country" (([S][S])[A][−A]) are classified as [X][A][−A] ([X]=[S][S]). Related discussions can be found inthe above section; and below, a short comparison of these cases.

For the [S][A][S][−A] pattern, examples like:

争长论短 *zheng1/fight_for chang2/long lun4/argue duan3/short* "to argue for something",
挑肥拣瘦 *tiao1/select fei2/fat jian3/pick shou4/slim* "to pick out the best and leave the rest",
摇头摆尾 *yao2/shake tou2/head bai3/sway wei3/tail* "shaking one's body".
For the [A][S][−A][S] pattern, examples like:
朝思暮想 *zhao1/morning si1/think_of mu4/evening xiang3/miss* "to miss someone or something all the days",
前呼后拥 *qian1/front hu1/endorse hou4/after you1/support* "to be surrounded and supported by many people",
左拥右抱 *zuo3/right yong1/support you4/left bao4/hug* "to have beauties in both arms".

And, very few cases can be in both structures, like:

昏天暗地hun1/dusky tian1/sky an4/dark di4/earth = 天昏地暗 tian1/sky hun1/dusky di4/earth an4/dark, both mean "in a state of pure darkness".
Moreover, in some of the cases, the synonym pairing can be picked out to combine a compound of coordinate construction. For example:
撩是斗非 *liao2/provoke shi4/right dou4/fight fei1/wrong* = 撩斗是非 *liao2/provoke dou4/fight shi4/right fei1/wrong* "to provoke a quarrel",
左顾右盼 *zuo3/right gu4/look you4/left pan4/watch* = 左右顾盼 *zuo3/right you4/left gu4/look pan4/watch* "to look around",
生离死别 *sheng1/alive li2/depart si3/dead bie2/separate* = 生死离别 *sheng2/alive si3/dead li2/depart bie2/separate* "to say goodbye and may never see each again".

They are all in the pattern of [A][−A][S][S] or [S][S][A][−A].

Additionally, in some of the examples, positions [1][2] and [3][4] can be shifted without meaning changing, like:

天长地久 *tian1/sky chang2/long di4/earth jiu3/long_time* = 地久天长 *di4/earth jiu3/long_time tian1/sky chang2/long* "a very long time".

But usually the ordering of the opposite pairing members; that is, the ones which take the prior places, still follows the rules we summarize in Sect. 3.4. In order words, *tian1chang2di4jiu3* is more preferred than *di4jiu3tian1chang2*.

In Sect. 3.3.2, we talked about [A][−A][X] and [X][A][−A] patterns. The [A][−A][X] pattern includes telescope compounds like 南北极 *nan2/south bei3/north ji2/pole* "south and north poles", and other compounds like 起落架 *qi3/up luo4/down jia4/frame* "undercarriage", 买卖婚姻 *mai3/buy mai4/sell hun1yin1/marriage* "marriage for purchase", 众寡悬殊 *zhong4/mass gua3/few xuan1/different shu1/extremely* "a great gap in numerical strength". The [X][A][−A] pattern has examples like 争高低 *zheng1/fight_for gao1/high di1/low* "fight it out", 跑买卖 *pao3/run mai3/buy mai4/sell* "travelling for business", 享誉中外 *xiang3/enjoy yu4/fame zhong1/China wai4/abroad*, "all over the body", 结发夫妻 *jie2/bind fa4/hair fu1/husband qi1/wife* "husband and wife of the first marriage".

So, what are the differences between these two patterns and the ones in this section? Do they overlap?

The answer to this question depends on whether the examples of [X][A][−A] or [A][−A][X] can be shifted to [S][A][S][−A] or [A][S][−A][S], without changing their meanings.

For the blend/contraction compounds: 南北极 *nan2/south bei3/north ji2/pole* ➔ 南极北极 *nan2/south ji2/pole bei3/north ji2/pole* ([A][X][−A][X]). It is acceptable, but the *nan2ji2bei3ji2* may be better seen as a coordination of two compounds, rather than a compound of coordination construction.

For the non-blend/contraction compounds: 起落架 *qi3/up luo4/down jia4/frame* ➔* 起架落架 *qi3/up jia4/frame luo4/down jia4/frame*. The latter saying is not acceptable in Chinese, for the meaning of "undercarriage".

For 买卖婚姻 *mai3/buy mai4/sell hun1yin1/marriage* and 众寡悬殊 *zhong4/mass gua3/few xuan1/different shu1/extremely*, neither of the saying of 买婚姻卖婚姻 *mai3/buy hun1yin1/marriage mai4/sell hun1yin1/marriage* nor 众悬殊寡悬殊 *zhong4/mass xuan1/different shu1/extremelygua3/few xuan1/different shu1/extremely* is acceptable, since "mercenary" (*mai3mai4*) is used as a whole to modify "marriage" (*hun1yin1*), and, "extreme difference" (*xuan2shu1*) is for the gap between "many" (*zhong4*) and "few" (*gua3*).

For 争高低 *zheng1/compete_for gao1/high di1/low* ➔? 争高争低 *zheng1/compete_for gao1/high zheng1/compete_for di1/low* "fight it out", 跑买卖 *pao3/run mai3/buy mai4/sell* ➔? 跑买跑卖 *pao3/run mai3/buy pao3/run mai4/sell* "travelling for business", the new ones are understandable for native speakers, but are not as naturally used as the previous ones. Even for the ones which can be shifted into the [X][A][X][−A] or [A][X][−A][X] pattern, it is sometimes more natural to have the doubled member replaced with a synonym, like 争高低 *zheng1/compete_for gao1/high di1/low* ➔? 争高争低 *zheng1/compete_for gao1/high zheng1/fight_for di1/low* ([X][A][X][−A])➔争高抢低[8] *zheng1/compete_for gao1/high qiang3/rob di1/low* ([S][A][S][−A]). That is similar to the cases mentioned in Sect. 3.2, which are marked as [A][−A][S][S] (左右顾盼 *zuo3/right you4/left gu4/look pan4/watch*, 生死离别 *sheng2/alive si3/dead li2/depart bie2/separate*) or [S][S][A][A] (征战南北 *zheng1/conquer zhan4/fight nan2/south bei3/north*, 欺瞒上下 *qi1/cheat man2/conceal shang4/up xia4/down*, 撩斗是非 *liao2/provoke dou4/fight shi4/right fei1/wrong*).

[8] *Zheng1gao1qiang3di1* is a partially-directed compound. The meaning of *qiang3di1*, 'to rob for lowness', is not accepted and therefore it is ignored. The real meaning of the compound is still 'to fight for being higher (or, better position)', which is the same as *zheng1gao1di1*.

For 享誉中外 *xiang3/enjoy yu4/fame zhong1/China wai4/abroad*, the sayings of *享誉中享誉外 *xiang3/enjoy yu4/fame zhong1/China xiang3/enjoy yu4/fame wai4/abroad* is unacceptable.

Above are examples of the [X][A][−A] or [A][−A][X] pattern that cannot be changed into [X][A][−A] or [A][−A][X], except for contraction compounds and ones like *zheng1gao1di1* or *pao3mai3mai4*.

As a whole, hit numbers show that it is more preferred to have [S][A][S][−A] (216 hits) than [A][S][−A][S′] (129 hits), [S][A][S′][−A] (118 hits), or [A][S][−A][S] (17 hits).

3.3.5 Opposite Frames

The most common frames in our data are generalized as following:

Complementary Frames

[阳][X][阴][Y], [阴][X][阳][Y]: 阳奉阴违 *yang2/Yang feng4/support yin1/Yin wei2/opposite* "to support in public but opposite in secret", 阴盛阳衰 *yin1/Yin sheng4/prosperous yang2/Yang shuai1/decline* "females are more overwhelming males";
[X][生][Y][死], [死][X][活][Y]: 出生入死 *chu1/out sheng1/life ru4/in si3/death* "to take great risk", 死去活来 *si3/death qu4/go huo2/life lai2/come* "hovering between life and death";
[有][X][无][Y]: 有增无减 *you3/have zeng1/increase wu2/no jian3/decrease* "increasing", 有去无回 *you3/have qu4/come wu2/no hui2/return* "one way trip".

Antonym Frames

[先][X][后][Y], [前][X][后][Y], [X][前][Y][后], [X][先][Y][后]: 先难后易 *xian1/first nan2/difficult hou3/then yi3/easy* "to first solve the most difficult problems", 前仆后继 *qian2/before pu1/fall_forward hou4/after ji4/continue* "one falls but the followings continue", 争先恐后 *zheng1/struggle xian1/front kong3/afraid hou3/behid* "to struggle to be the first and fear to be left behind";
[内][X][外][Y], [外][X][内][Y], [X][里][Y][外]: 内忧外患 *nei4/inside you1/disturbance wai4/outside huan4/problem* "having problems from both inside and outside", 外驰内张 *wai4/outside chi2/relax nei4/inside zhang1/tense* "to pretend being relax but keep tense", 吃里扒外 *chi1/eat li3/inside pa2/support wai4/outside* "to secretly support the opponent of one's supporter";
[重][X][轻][Y]: 重文轻武 *zhong4/overrate wen2/arts qing1/underrate wu3/military* "to pay more attentions on arts than military";
[X][多][Y][少]: 僧多粥少 *seng1/monk duo1/many zhou1/porridge shao3/few* "too many monks share too little food", 男多女少 *nan2/male duo1/many nv3/female shao3/few* "more men than women";

[大][X][小][Y]: 大同小异 *da4/big tong2/same xiao3/little yi4/different* “to be the same in large picture while keep variations in details”, 大惊小怪 *da4/big jing1/fuss xiao3/little guai4/surprise* “make a fuss about trifles”;
[老][X][少][Y]: 老夫少妻 *lao3/old fu1/husband shao4/young qi1/wife* “old husband with young wife”;
[上][X][下][Y], [X][上][Y][下]: 上行下效 *shang4/up xing2/work xia4/down xiao4/copy* “subordinates follows the way of superiors”, 欺上瞒下 *qi1/cheat shang4/up man2/defraud xia4/down* “to cheat people arounds”;
[长][X][短][Y], [X][长][Y][短]: 长吁短叹 *chang2/long yu1/moan duan3/short tan4/groan* “to sigh incessantly”, 情长纸短 *qing2/love chang2/long zhi3/paper duan3/short* “the paper is too short to write down all my love”;
[厚][X][薄][Y]: 厚古薄今 *hou4/thick gu3/ancient bo2/thin jin1/today* “to overrate the past while underrate the present”;
[左][X][右][Y]: 左思右想 *zuo3/left si1/think you4/right xiang3/consider* “to think twice”;
[明][X][暗][Y]: 明查暗访 *ming2/bright cha2/explore an4/dark fang3/invest* “to invest in public and private”;
[好][X][歹][Y]: 好说歹说 *hao3/good shuo1/say dai3/bad shuo1/say* “to persuade in many ways”.

Converse Frames

[此][X][彼][Y], [X][此][Y][彼]: 此起彼伏 *ci3/here qi3/up bi3/there fu2/down* “to rise one over another”, 非此即彼 *fei1/not ci3/here ji2/BE bi3/there* “one or the other”;
[X][来][Y][往], [X][来][Y][去], [X][去][Y][来]: 寒来暑往 *han2/cold lai2/come shu3/hot wang3/go* “from winter to summer”, 冬去春来 *dong1/winter qu4/go chun1/spring lai2/come* “the end of winter and the coming of spring”.
[出][X][入][Y]: 出将入相 *chu1/out jiang4/general ru4/in xiang4/prime_minister* “being in a high position”, 出生入死 *chu1/out sheng1/life ru4/in si4/death* “to take great risk”.

Taxonomy Frames

[天][X][地][Y], [X][天][Y][地]: 天宽地阔 *tian1/sky kuan1/wide di4/earth kuo4/broad* “a wide world”, 顶天立地 *ding3/touch tian1/sky li4/stand_on di4/earth* “gigantic”;
[南][X][北][Y], [X][南][Y][北]: 南来北往 *nan2/south lai2/come bei3/north wang3/go* “a traffic from different places”, 天南海北 *tian1/sky nan2/south hai3/sea bei3/north* “a long distance”;
[东][X][西][Y]: 东成西就 *dong1/east cheng2/achievement xi1/west jiu4/acquirement* “a great achivenment”;
[X][古][Y][今]; [古][X][今][Y]: 博古通今 *bo2/go_through gu3/ancient tong1/go_through jin1/today* “know everything”, 古往今来 *gu3/ancient wang3/go jin1/today lai2/come* “all the times”;

[横][X][竖][Y]: 横眉竖眼 *heng2/horizontal mei2/eye_brow shu4/stand yang3/eye* "to glare with anger";
[X][头][Y][尾]: 藏头露尾 *cang2/hide tou2/head lu4/show wei3/tail* "to hide the head bu show the tail".

We have to point out that the members which can appear in such frames are generally (or, gradually) considered as (pragmatic) opposites as well, if they were not in logical meanings. In fact, we may guess that the taxonomy pairings somehow generate by first entering such pairings then be used in pairs to refer (pragmatic) contrast in language. For example:

古往今来 *gu3/ancient wang3/go jin1/nowadays lai2/come* "all the times"

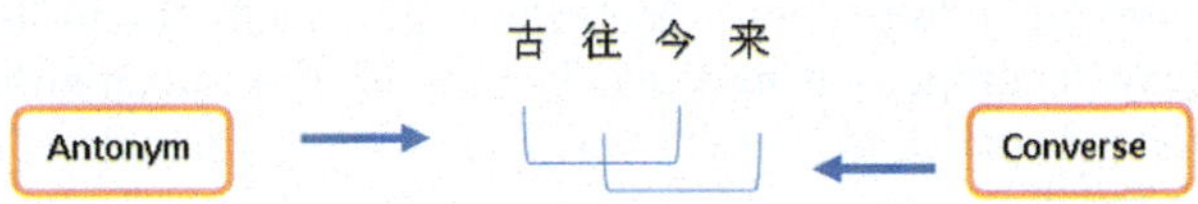

In this example, *wang3* and *lai2* are a converse pair; and *gu2* and *jin1*, an antonym pair. The two pairs together mean "all the time (from the ancient to nowadays)".

南来北往 *nan1/south lai2/come bei3/north wang3/go* "a traffic from different places"

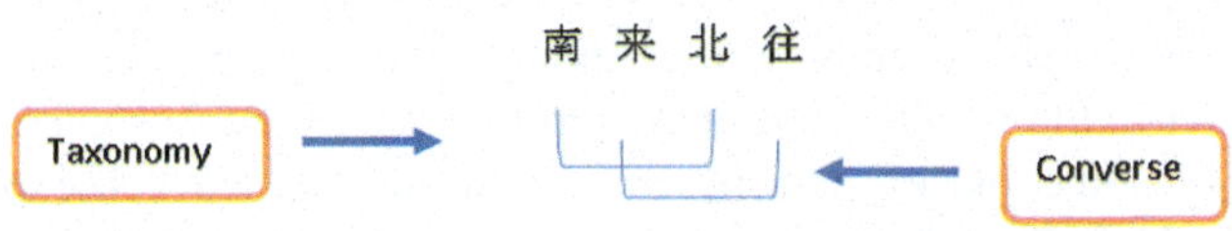

天南海北 *tian1/sky nan2/south hai3/sea bei3/north* "a long distance"

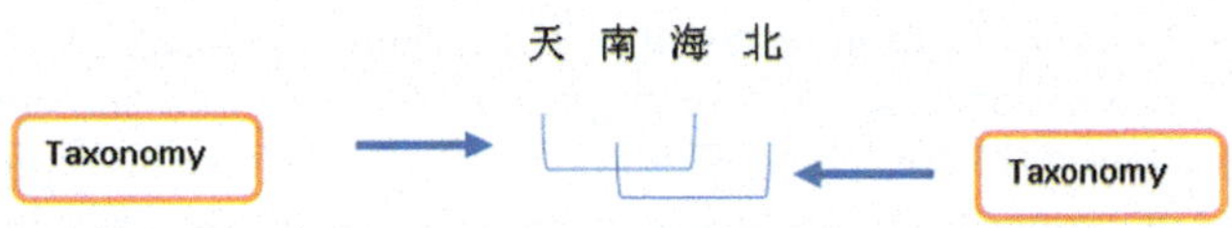

3.4 Discussion

3.4.1 Functions of Opposite Compounds

[A][−A] and Its Derived Patterns

For the [A][−A] pattern, the functions of such compounds usually are to cover the whole scale, or to emphasize the two points of the scale.

Some of the opposite combinations refer to the property they belong to, like 轻重 *qing1/light zhong4/heavy* "weight", 长短 *chang2/long duan3/short* "length":

(36) 这两个包裹轻重不一样.

zhe4/this liang3/two ge4/CL bao1guo3/packageqing1/light zhong4/heavy bu4/not yi1yang4/same
"The weights of the two packages are different."

(37) 比较两根彩带的长短

bi3jiao4/compare liang3/two gen1/CL cai3/color dai4/belt de0/DE chang2/long duan3/short
"to compare the lengths of the two color belts"

Other similar examples include, 快慢 *kuai4/fast man4/slow* "speed", and, 松紧 *song1/loose jin3/tight* "tightness". Such cases are usually found in the category of an antonym. Such compounds may also be used to measure an abstract concept. 长短 *chang2/long duan3/short* "length" in the following example is used to measure the length of time:

(38) 餐桌的高度影响食客停留时间长短

can1zhuo1/dining_table de0/DE gao1du4/height ying1xiang3/effect shi2ke4/customer ting2liu2/stay shi2jian1/time chang2/long duan3/short
"the height of dining table effect the staying time of customers"

For converse pairing verbs, the combination of two pairing members is more likely to refer to the whole event involving the actions. For instance, 来 *lai2* means "to come to some place" and 往 *wang3* means "to leave the place". For the compound of 来往 *lai2wang3*, we have expressions like 和某人来往 *he2/with mo3ren2/someone lai2/come wang3/go* "to make friends with someone", 来往车辆 *lai2/come wang3/go che1liang4/vehicle* "traffic", 来往账户 *lai2/come wang3/go zhang4hu4/account* "current account". The compound 来往 *lai2wang3* means "contact (with someone) or visit (some place)". Contact/visit and come/go are in a metonymy relation (Cruse 1986; Miller et al. 1993). That means, come/go is part of the activity of "contacting" or "visiting". But as can be seen in Chinese, we have *lai2* and *wang3* combined to refer to the whole activity of "contacting someone" or "visiting someplace":

(39) 他们家<u>来往</u>的都是生意场上的人.

ta1men0/they jia1/home lai2/come wang3/go de0/DE dou1/all shi4/be sheng1yi4/business chang3/field shang4/on de0/DE ren2/people
"Their families are only in touch with business people."

Sometimes, the word order is reversed in order to satisfy the prosody:

(40) 往来港澳通行证

wang3/go lai2/come gang3/Hong_Kong ao4/Macau tong1xing2zheng4/passport
"passport (for Mainland resident) to Hong Kong and Macau"

The same function is also found in other converse pairings such as 嫁娶 *jia4/marriage (from females' aspect) qv3/marriage (from males' aspect)* "marriage", 伸缩 *shen1/elongate suo1/curtail* "to elongate and/or to curtail", 问答 *wen4/ask da2/answer* "ask and answer". Moreover, some complementary pairings also have the similar function, like 死活 *si3/dead huo2/alive* in 死活不答应 *si3/dead huo2/alive bu4/not da1ying4/agree* "do not agree in anyway".

Some taxonomy compounds also have the same function. 甘苦 *gan1/sweet ku3/bitter* is another case. Derived from the five most common tastes 酸甜苦辣咸 *suan1/sour tian2/sweet ku3/bitter la4/spicy xian2/salty*, each of them is supposed to contrast with all the rest of the four flavors in taste. Moreover, the saying of 甘苦自知 *gan1/sweet ku3/bitter zi4/oneself zhi1/know* can be translated as "only the wearer knows where the shoes hurt", where 甘苦 *gan1/sweet ku3/bitter* together cover the mixed and unspeakable taste (of life). These ones are considered to refer to the **hypernym**, under which the taxonomies lie on.

As to the color terms, 黑 *hei1/black* and 白 *bei2/white* are two single colors but often used to refer to a whole domain of color, especially in metaphor:

(41) 警察不分黑白就把在场的人都抓了起来.

jing3cha2/policeman bu4/not fen1/distinguish hei1/black bei2/white jiu4/JIU ba3/BA zai4chang3/be_present de0/DE ren2/people dou1/all zhua1/arrest le0/LE qi3lai2/up

"The policeman arrested all the people in presence without distinguishing who is suspicious and who is not."

Meanwhile, some converse pairings only refer to the two arguments of the relationship, for example, 主宾 *zhu3/host bin1/guest* "host and guest", 夫妻 *fu1/husband qi1/wife* "husband and wife", 敌友 *di2/enemy you3/friend* "enemy and friend", 父母 *fu4/father mu3/mother* "father and mother".

Some compounds refer to the two members in some cases, while in other situations they would refer to the whole scale: 老少 *lao3/old you4/young* "the elders and the youngsters" and 老少皆宜 *lao3/old you4/young jie1/all yi2/suitable* "being suitable for all ages".

For taxonomy words, such usage is more common. 水 *shui3/water* and 火 *huo3/fire* is another pair of taxonomies, and they are often used together to symbolize a contrast relationship, such as, 水火不容 *shui3/water huo3/fire bu4/not rong2/compatible* "incompatible as water and fire", 势如水火 *shi4/situation ru2/like shui3/water huo3/fire* "to be hostile".

文 *wen2/civil* and 武 *wu3/military* are the two departments in traditional Chinese government. 文官 *wen2/civil guan1/official* "civil servant" are the ones recruited originally by competition selections, which are usually in the form of writing. On the other hand, 武官 *wu3/military guan1/official* "military official" are the ones like generals, colonels and commanders. 文武百官 *wen2/civil wu3/military bai3/hundred guan1/official* means "all the official in the government". Besides, *wen2* and *wu3* are also used as the properties of one person, such as in 文武双全

wen2/civil wu3/military shuang1/two quan2/complete "well educated in civilization and well trained in military arts".

In Chinese, compared with *wu3*, *wen2* is considered to be more modest. Therefore, *wen2* sometimes is used as the synonym of mild, and *wu3* as the synonym of strong or violent. The idiom 文武并用 *wen2/civil wu3/military bing4/together yong4/use* "to use carrot and stick policy" is commonly used in describing a balanced management system.

The differences in degree between *wen2* and *wu3*, as two kinds of properties, sometimes are used similarly for the antonym pair*da4: xiao4* ("big: small"). Thus in Chinese people may say 文火 *wen2/civil huo3/fire* referring to "mild fire", and 武火 *wu3/military huo3/fire* referring to "heavy fire".

These above instances are the compounds which refer to two points of the scales, or, to two members of the taxonomy.

The general tendency is that, for [A][−A] patterns, all the compounds (at least in our data), no matter which category they belong to, fall into the function of covering the whole scale, or of emphasizing the two points. Complementary compounds are the representation of the two points/members. But for antonym pairings, it is both likely to have the compounds referring to the whole scale – as representing their property – or, to refer to the two extreme points. And for converse pairings, many of them refer to the hypernym which is the event containing the two actions or relations. The situation of taxonomy is more close to that of the antonym.

The derived patterns of [A][−A] pattern, that is, [A][−A][A][−A], [A] [A][−A] [−A], [A][−A][A] and [A][−A][−A][A], can be considered as the emphasized forms of the basic [A][−A] pattern. And the functions of such patterns are the same: to cover all the possible situations on/around the scale and to emphasis the overall coverage.

[A][−A][X] and Its Derived Patterns

高低 *gao1/high di1/low* in 争高低 *zheng1/compete_for gao1/high di1/low*, "fight it out", for example, emphasizes the two extreme points of the scale. In other words, to emphasize the difference in level of the two competing sides, no matter how close they are in absolute quantity. In this case, *zheng1gao1di1* is equal to that of 争输赢 *zheng1/compete_for shu1/failure ying2/victory* "fight it out" or 争雌雄 *zheng1/compete_for ci2/female xiong2/male* "fight it out". Different from *gao1:di1*, both *shu1:ying2* and *ci2:xiong2* are complementaries, which represent the assumption of "if not A, then B". So, in this compound of *zheng1gao1di1*, *gao1di1* is used as a pair of complementary (ungradable) but not of antonym (gradable).

The converse pair of *mai3mai4*, again, as it does in [A][−A] pattern, refers to the event of "doing business", by combining the action of buying and selling. Another converse pair of *fu1qi1*, "husband and wife", is not the same case. 夫妻店 *fu1/husband qi1/wife1dian4/store* means "the store which is managed by a couple", refers to the relation of being a couple; 夫妻相 *fu1/husband qi1/wife xiang4/face* means "similar appearances (of a couple)", refers to the similarity of their appearances; and, 夫妻树 *fu1/husband qi1/wife shu4/tree* is the trees whose branches and/or roots are twisted, symbolizing their close relation.

Zhong1wai4 in 中外对话 *zhong1/China wai4/abroad dui4hua4/dialogue*, "dialogue between China and outside", 中外合作 *zhong1/China wai4/abroad he2zuo4/co-operate*, "co-operation between China and other countries", separates China from the rest of the world, as a single independent country; meanwhile, in 享誉中外 *xiang3/enjoy yu4/reputation zhong1/China wai4/abroad*, it means "the whole world", China and the other countries, as one part.

Shang4xia4 is used to complement the meaning of *hun2shen1*, but may not be used alone to replace *hun2shen1*:

(42) 浑身没带一毛钱

hun2/all shen1/body mei2/no dai4/bring yi1/one mao2/CL qian2/money
"do not bring any money"

(43) 浑身上下没带一毛钱

hun2/all shen1/body shang4/up xia4/down mei2/no dai4/bring yi1/one mao2/CL qian2/money
"do not bring any money"

(44) ? 上下没带一毛钱

shang4/up xia4/down mei2/no dai4/bring yi1/one mao2/CL qian2/money
"do not bring any money"

Hence, the functions of these patterns are generalized as follow:

First, to cover all the scales in three approaches:

The opposite pairing is used to modify the noun, like: 起落架 *qi3/up luo4/down jia4/frame* "undercarriage", 买卖婚姻 *mai3/buy mai4/sell hun1yin1/marriage* "marriage for purchase", 结发夫妻 *jie2/bind fa4/hair fu1/husband qi1/wife* "husband and wife of the first marriage"; or, to be limited by the noun, like: 浑身上下 *hun2/all shen1/body shang4/up xia4/down* "from top to down"; or, to be the complement of the verb, like: 争高低 *zheng1/compete_for gao1/high di1/low* "fight it out", 跑买卖 *pao3/run mai3/buy mai4/sell* "travelling for business", 享誉中外 *xiang3/enjoy yu4/reputation zhong1/China wai4/abroad* "enjoy an excellent reputation at home and abroad".

Secondly, to emphasize the two extreme points, the meaning of such compounds is dependent on the linking words, like: 老来少 *lao3/old lai2/become shao4/young* "an old man with a young heart", 供大于求 *gong4/support da4/large yu2/than qiu2/order* "oversupply", 自上而下 *zi4/from shang4/up er2/to xia4/down* "from top to bottom".

[A1] [−A1] and [A2][−A2]

The functions of this pattern are usually limited to two basic ones: first, emphasize the one polar of the opposite scale. The pattern doubles the same meaning, both by positively asserting it (凶 *xiong1/misfortune* 多 *duo1/many*) and by negating the opposite one (吉 *ji2/fortune* 少 *shao3/few*). Similar cases are: 优胜劣汰 *you1/good sheng4/win lie4/bad tai4/eliminate* "survival of the best", 贪生怕死 *tan1/seek_after sheng1/life pa4/be_afraid_of si3/death* "be afraid of death". The two parts ([A1]

[A2]; [−A1][−A2]) are sharing the same meanings, and therefore the logical reading of the whole compound would not interrupted with either of them missed.

The case of 弃暗投明 *qi4/dump an4/dark tou2/head_to ming2/bright*, "to resign from the criminal group and join a justice one", may be less typical in this sense; that is to say, the meaning of *qi4* does not necessarily infer that of *tou2*, and *qi4an4* is not logically equal to *tou2ming2*. Since *qi4* and *tou2* can be treated as two separated and not dependent verbs, *qi4an4tou2ming2* may also be argued as a **serial verb construction** (连动结构), rather than a **coordinate construction** (并列结构). The same dilemma is also applicable to that of 低买高卖 *di1/low mai3/buy gao1/high mai4/sell* "to buy at a low price and sell at a high price", 得小失大 *de2/gain xiao3/small shi1/lose da4/big* "to lose a big benefit for gaining a small one", 截长补短 *jie2/cut chang2/long bu3/complete duan3/short* "to use the strong point to cover the weakness" and so on. That is because the converse pairings, unlike the ones of complementary, do not carry logical dependence within the two pairing members. The existence of one member, sometimes, does not require that of the other one.

Secondly, for the other examples like, 早出晚归 *zao3/early chu2/out wan3/night gui1/return* "get out early and return late", 知易行难 *zhi1/know yi4/easy xing2/act nan2/difficult* "easy to know but hard to do" and so on, the opposite pairings are placed together to emphasize the contrast between the two parts. In the first place, within these pairings, there is no logical inference between two parts. For example, *zao3chu1* does not necessarily mean *wan3gui1* in logics; secondly, *zao3chu1* and *wan3gui1* together strengthen the meaning that the subject who does so must work a long time (everyday). Hence, neither of the two parts can be ignored in completing the meaning of the whole compound.

[A][−A] and Synonym Pairings

In most of the cases, the opposite pairing is used to modify the synonym pairing, and, the synonym pairing is used to doubly emphasize the overlapped meaning of the two pairing members. For example, 挑肥拣瘦 *tiao1/pick fei2/fat jian3/choose shou4/thin* means "be picky"; 同甘共苦 *tong2/together gan1/sweet gong4/together ku3/bitter* means "sharing the same situation (no matter good or bad)", 朝思暮想 *zhao1/morning si1/think mu4/evening xiang3/miss* means "missing someone or something all the time (day and night)"; 天寒地冻 *tian1/sky han2/cold di4/earth dong4/freezing* means "outside (sky and land) being cold".

However, some cases focus on the partial meaning of compounds. For example, 寻死 *xun2/seek si3/*death and 觅活 *mi4/seek huo2/alive* together mean "wanting to die" (*xun2si3*) but not "seeking to live" (*mi4huo2*). Similar cases include 救亡图存 *jiu4/save wang2/death tu2/for cun2/living* "to struggle for survival (of a nation or a race)". These words are called **partially-directed compounds** (偏义复词). Previous studies (He and Jiang 1980; Luo 2012, among others) pointed out that usually it is the negative part, not the positive one, representing the core meaning of the whole compound.

Logic Standard of Functions and Common Frames

We employ a logic standard to explain the functions of patterns. Logic cannot explain all the possible situations in natural language. But using logical standards at least provides a consistent categorization to the study. The basic functions of these structures are divided on the logical basis:

a. Normal Scale (to cover every member of the whole scale):

For examples,

[有][A][有][−A]: 有始有终 *you3/have shi3/beginning you3/have zhong1/end* "to have something finished";
[可][A][可][−A]: 可有可无 *ke3/can_be you3/have ke3/can_be wu2/not_have* "the issue is not important";
[从][A][到/至][−A]: 从古至今 *cong2/from gu3/ancient_times zhi4/to jin1/nowadays* "in all ages";
[自][A][而][−A]: 自上而下 *zi4/from shang4/up er2/to xia4/down* "from up to down";
[由][A][及][−A]: 由表及里 *you2/from biao3/surface ji2/to li3/inside* "from surface to inside";
[A][A][−A][−A]: 来来往往 *lai1/come lai1/come wang3/leave wang3/leave* "come and go";
[A][V][−A][V]: 东想西想 *dong1/east xiang3/think xi1/west xiang3/think* "to consider very carefully";
[V][A][V][−A]: 死说活说 *si3/dead shuo1/speak huo2/alive shuo1/speak* "to try every ways to persuade (someone)";

[A1][A2][−A1][−A2]: 是非黑白 *shi4/right fei1/wrong hei1/black bai2/white* "rights and wrongs", 天南海北 *tian1/sky nan2/south hai3/sea bei3/north* "all over the world".

b. Middle Scale (to refer to the middle of the scale, and/or negate or ignore the two extreme points):

For examples,

[不][A][不][−A]: 不卑不亢 *bu4/no bei1/servile bu4/no kang4/overbearing* "be neither servile nor overbearing";
[半][A][半][−A]: 半开半闭 *ban4/half kai1/open ban4/half bi4/closed* "half open";
[半][A][不][−A]: 半死不活 *ban4/half si3/dead bu4/no huo2/alive* "half dead".

c. Extreme Points (to emphasize the two poles of the scale, and negate or ignore the middle of the scale):

For examples,

[大][A][大][−A]: 大是大非 *da4/big shi4/right da4/big fei1/wrong* "the question of principles";
[A][−A][分明]: 爱憎分明 *ai4/love zeng4/hate fen1ming2/distinguished* "be distinguished to whom love and whom hate";
[时][A][时][−A]: 时冷时热 *shi2/sometimes leng3/cold shi2/sometimes re4/hot* "sometimes cold and sometimes hot".

In this case, there can be two sub-kinds of functions: one is used to indicate the two points of the scale, where they can occur at the same time; while the other is used to indicate the incompatibility of the two points, which cannot both occur in the same situation, such as:

[非][A][即][−A]: 非此即彼 *fei1/not ci3/this ji2/be bi3/that* "either-or";
[是][A][是][−A]: 是好是坏 *shi4/be hao3/good shi4/be huai4/bad* "be good or bad";
[或][A][或][−A]: 或大或小 *huo4/or da4/big huo4/or xiao3/small* "either big or small".

d. Marked Point (to emphasize one of the two extreme points and negate the other one):

For examples,
[A1][A2][−A1][−A2]:

聚少离多 *jv4/get_together shao3/less li2/depart duo1/more* "more departed than get-together",
否极泰来 *pi3/bad_luck ji2/end tai4/good_luck lai2/come* "bad luck ends and good luck succeeds",
优胜劣汰 *you1/good sheng4/win lie4/bad tai4/eliminate* "survival of the best".

Beyond Logical Standards
However, language is not mathematics. It does not operate only with logic. There are also some functions beyond the explanation of logic and these occur very frequently in our research, such as:

e. Scale Changing:

For examples,
[化/转][A][为][−A]: 转败为胜 *zhuan3/turn bai4/defeat wei2/be sheng4/victory* "turn defeat into victory", 化敌为友 *hua4/change di2/enemy wei2/be you3/friend* "convert enemies into friends".

f. Under Specialized:

For examples,

[似][A][似][−A]: 似有似无 *si4/like you3/have si4/like wu/not_have* "intangible";
[若][A][若][−A]: 若隐若现 *ruo4/like yin3/disappear ruo4/like xian4/appear* "intangible";
[似][A][若][−A]: 似有若无 *si4/like you3/have ruo4/like wu2/not_have* "intangible";
[乍][A][乍][−A]: 乍暖还寒 *zha4/just nuan3/warm huan2/still han2/cold* "(the weather) be just warming up but still cold".

For the cases like 前仆后继 *qian2/front pu1/fall hou4/after ji4/continue* "endless people devote themselves to doing something", 承上启下 *cheng2/hold shang4/up qi3/open xia4/down* "being the connection between the preceding and the following", their functions may be called:

g. Eventual Expression.

3.4.2 Order Within Constructions

Within these above constructions, it is interesting to see whether there are any principles in deciding the word ordering within the constructions.

Semantic factor is always considered as an important one. **Pollyanna Principle** (Matlin and Stang 1978) points out that, the positive are preferred to be placed in the front of the negative ones. And this theory is supported by Chinese studies (Tang 1979; Xu 2000). For example, Tang (1979) mentioned that the ones baring positive or unmarked (or, neutral) meaning are preferred to take the prior position. Hence, the word order of "antonymous coordinate construction" (1979: 18) is featured as having the positive meaning one in front position and the negative one, in the latter position. That is because the positive one usually bores the neutral or unmarked meaning. The unmarked meaning is preferred in order than the marked one.

Additionally, he (1979: 20–26) lists out fifteen special word orders in Chinese, such as:

(1) “天” > “人” (the concept of *tian1* “sky” prior to that of *ren2* “human being”)
(2) “人” > “兽”或”物” (the concept of *ren2* “human being” prior to that of *shou4* “animal” or *wu4* “things”)
(3) “公” > “私” (the concept of *gong1* “public” prior to that of *si1* “private”)
(4) “家” > “人” (the concept of *jia1* “family” prior to that of *ren2* “human being”)
(5) “长” > “幼” (the concept of *zhang3* “senior” prior to that of *you4* “junior”)
(6) “尊” > “卑” (the concept of *zun1* “respected” prior to that of *bei1* “humble”)
(7) “亲” > “疏” (the concept of *qin1* “close” prior to that of *shu1* “distant”)
(8) “男” > “女” (the concept of *nan2* “male” prior to that of *nv3* “female”)
(9) “优” > “劣” (the concept of *you1* “good(_quantity)” prior to that of *lie4* “bad (_quantity)”)
(10) “盈” > “亏” (the concept of *ying2* “surplus” prior to that of *kui1* “deficit”)
(11) “主” > “副” (the concept of *zhu3* “host” prior to that of *ke4* “guest”)
(12) “鸟” > “(鱼)兽” (the concept of *niao3* “avifauna” prior to that of *yu2* “ichthyfauna” or *shou4* “quadrupled”)
(13) “上” > “下” (the concept of *shang4* “up” prior to that of *xia4* “down”)
(14) “软” > “硬”(或者, ”流体” > “固体”) (the concept of *ruan3* “soft” prior to that of *ying4* “hard”, or, *liu2ti3*“ liquid” prior to that one of *gu4ti3* “solid”)
(15) “里”(”进”) > “外” (”出”) (the concept of *li3* “inside” prior to that of *wai4* “outside”, or, *jin4* “come in” prior to that of *chu1* “go out”)

However, this theory is only partly supported by Ding and Huang (2014). Their studying on the 218 bi-syllabic opposite compounds in [A][−A] construction suggests that Pollyanna Principle is not sufficient to explain all the cases in the data. Firstly, Pollyanna Principle is not applicable to all the compounds. Converse compounds, like 往返 *wang3/go fan3/return*, cannot be applied with such a principle. Converse compound orders are actually decided by temporal order, which means the order of happening of events. So 返 *fan3/return* cannot because be placed in front of 往 *wang3/go*, since the event of “going out” should happen before the one of “returning”. And, when there is no temporal difference between the two components, the compounds prefer to agree on the positive-in-front order.

Secondly, Prosodic factor is also supported by previous studies such as Chen and Yu (1979), Zhou (1985). The basic assumption is that the order of Chinese bisyllabic compounds is organized by tone orders. For that, Ding and Huang (2014) computed the tone[9] order of the 218 [A][−A] compounds and the results showed as below (Table 3.2).

[9]Because of the limitation of time and knowledge, this paper only considers the tone of each word when it is pronounced alone in modern Chinese. The tonal modification, which means the influence by neighboring words or the possible change in actual speaking, is not considered. From the aspect of historical linguistics, it is also important to keep in mind that pronunciation changes with time, so the tone of certain words in modern Chinese do not represent their tones in ancient time. That kind of change, however, is not discussed in this paper but is definitely interesting for study.

Table 3.2 Distribution of [A][−A] compounds with tone combination, from Ding and Huang (2014: 15)

In first position	In second position			
	1st tone	2nd tone	3rd tone	4th tone
1st tone	21	17	23	23
2nd tone	10	6	13	19
3rd tone	6	7	9	18
4th tone	5	12	3	26
Total: 218				

Table 3.3 Distribution of 82 examples with pollyanna principle and prosodic principle

Pollyanna principle	Prosodic principle	Example number
+	+	40
−	+	19
+	−	18
−	−	5
Total: 82		

Results show that 113 out of 218 examples having the prior tone is in first position; and 43 examples have the prior tone is in latter position; the rest 62 compounds have the same tone in both positions.

Moreover, 82[10] compounds which are both available to the Pollyanna Principle and prosodic principle: (Table 3.3)

So, in half of the cases (40 out of 82), the two principles do not clash.

Ding and Huang have not explained the cases in which these two principles disagree with each other and we further their study as follow.

19 examples are against the Pollyanna Principle but agree with the preferred prosodic principle, and they are:

(A1) 宾主 *bin1/guest zhu3/host*, 悲喜 *bei1/sad xi3/happy*, 枯荣 *ku1/withered rong2/flourishing*;
(A2) 冷热 *leng3/cold re4/hot*, 黑白 *hei1/black bai2/white*, 曲直 *qv1/curved zhi2/straight*, 贫富 *pin1/poor fu4/rich*;
(A3) 阴阳 *yin1/Yin yang2/Yang*, 刚柔 *gang1/hard rou2/soft*, 松紧 *song1/loose jin3/tight*, 出入 *chu1/out ru4/in*;
(A4) 苦乐 *ku3/bitter le4/happiness*, 虚实 *xv1/falsehood shi2/truth*, 输赢 *shu1/lose ying2/win*, 阴晴 *yin1/cloudy qing2/sunny*, 哀乐 *ai1/sad le4/happiness*, 疏密 *shu1/sparse mi4/dense*;
(A5) 难易 *nan2/difficult yi4/easy*, 轻重 *qing1/light zhong4/heavy*.

[10]Ding and Huang (2014) compute 84 compounds in this category. However, our latter examination shows, there are only 82 cases. The cases of 冷热 *leng3/cold re4/hot* and 苦乐 *ku3/bitter le4/happy* are wrongly accounted as the ones against both Pollyanna Principle and prosodic principle. Therefore, the total number should be 82.

At the same time, 18 examples agree with the Pollyanna Principle and are against preferred prosodic principle, and they are:

(B1) 主宾 *zhu3/host bin1/guest*, 喜悲 *xi3/happy bei1/sad*, 荣枯 *rong2/flourishing ku1/withered*;
(B2) 余缺 *yv2/surplus que1/be_short_of*, 有无 *you3/have wu2/lack*, 吉凶 *ji2/fortunate xiong1/unfortunate*, 得失 *de2/get shi1/lose*, 盈亏 *ying2/wax kui1/wane*, 奖罚 *jiang3/reward fa2/punish*, 赏罚 *shang3/reward fa2/punish*, 盛衰 *sheng4/prosperity shuai1/decline*, 厚薄 *hou4/thick bao2/thin*, 智愚 *zhi4/wise yv2/foolish*, 正邪 *zheng4/virtue xie2/evil*, 赚赔 *zhuan4/gain pei2/loss*, 大小 *da4/big xiao3/small*, 正反 *zheng4/positive fan3/negative*, 父母 *fu4/father mu3/mother*.

The rest 5 examples do not follow either of the two principles. They are:

(C1) 死生 *si3/deadsheng1/alive*, 死活 *si3/dead huo2/alive*, 短长 *duan3/short chang2/long*, 祸福 *huo4/unfortunate fu2/fortunate*;
(C2) 浊清 *zhuo2/muddy qing1/clear*.

The cases in (A1) and (A2) are sharing the same opposite pairings while the orders are reverse. For the two orders, 主宾 *zhu3bin1* and 荣枯 *rong2ku1* are more frequent than 宾主 *bin1zhu2* and 枯荣 *ku1rong2*. 悲喜 *bei1xi3* is more frequent than 喜悲 *xi3bei1*, but *bei1xi3* can not be replaced by *xi3bei1* in contexts. For example:

(45) 悲喜交加

bei1/sad xi3/happy jiao1/twist jia1/add
"having mixed feelings of grief and joy"
* 喜悲交加.
xi3/happy bei1/sad jiao1/twist jia1/add
"having mixed feelings of grief and joy"

The cases in (B1) are placing the unmarked (property) in prior position. For example, in *leng3re4*, *leng3* is placed in front of *re4* because the natural attribute of water is cold (*leng3*) while hot (*re4*) is not the natural but is the expected attribute:

(46) 冷热水交替浴

leng3/cold re4/hot shui3/water jiao1ti4/alternate yu4/bath
"a bath with alternation of cold and hot water"

Sometimes, 冷热 *leng3re4* is partially directed to the meaning of *leng3*, which is a metaphor of the dark side of things:

(47) 关心群众冷热全力迎峰度夏 (新华网)

guan1xin1/care qun2zhong4/people leng3/cold re4/hot quan2/all li4/power yin2/face feng1/peak du4/pass xia4/summer
"to care about the needs of people and be determined to pass the summer safely"

冷热 *leng3re4* in this sentence means the needs (caused by shortage) of people. And, for the same concept, another compound of 冷暖 *leng3/cold nuan3/warm* is found in the lexicon. Moreover, the above explanation is also applicable to the word ordering of *leng3nuan3*:

(48) 人情冷暖

ren1/people qing2/emotion leng3/cold nuan3/warm
"social snobbery"

Similar, 黑 *hei1/black* is the unmarked one in color domain rather than 白 *bai2/white*; 曲 *qv1/curved* is more common to see in natural and therefore it is the unmarked one rather than 直 *zhi1/straight*; and 贫 *pin1/poor*, not 富 *fu4/rich*, is unmarked because there are more poor peoples than rich ones. Hence, the cases in (B1) should be considered as in the order of unmarked-in-front.

Following Tang's list, we mark the cases in (C1) as negative-one-in-front (see Tang's rule 8, "male" prior to "female"; rule 14, "soft" prior to "hard"; and rule 15, "come in" prior to "go out"). However, our examples challenge these rules. They suggest that the concepts in front positions, in these compounds, may not be negative or culturally lower than the ones in later positions. Take 阴阳 *yin1yang2* "Yin and Yang" for example. The two concepts come from Daoism. 阴 *yin1/Yin* is often explained as feminine while 阳 *yang2/Yang* as masculine. The term "negative reaction" (in medicine) is translated as 阴性反应 *yin1xing4/negative fan3ying4/reaction*. *Yin1* stands for the "unchanged" result. In Daoism such concepts are considered to be the basic property of universe, that is, the unmarked ones. So when we refer to 男女 *nan2/male nv3/female*, in natural gender domain, it is *nan2* in front; but when refer to 阴阳 *yin1/Yin yang2/Yang*, in Daoism, it should always be *yin1* in front. Since there is not enough evidence to support Tang's rule 14, "soft" prior to "hard", it is hard to say 刚柔 *gang1/hard rou2/soft* and 松紧 *song1/loose jin3/tight* are against Pollyanna Principle. For 出入 *chu1/out ru4/in*, Tang's rule 15 defines that "come in" prior to "go out", but it is also possible to say *chu1/out* is departing oneself and *ru4/in* is moving to oneself, therefore it follows the same order as 往来 *wang3/go lai2/come* "come and go".

In (A4), we notice that the meaning of the compound, in contexts, refers to the meaning of the front character. For example, 输赢 *shu1/lose ying2/win:*

(49) 输赢不重要

shu1/lose ying2/win bu2/not zhong4yao4/important
"it is not important whether (you) win or lose"

The compound 输赢 *shu1/lose ying2/win* here is a neutral meaning of "result". For the rest cases in (A4), 苦乐 *ku3/bitter le4/happiness* refers to "tastes", 虚实 *xv1/falsehood shi2/truth* refers to "facts", 阴晴 *yin1/cloudy qing2/sunny* refers to "weathers" and 疏密 *shu1/sparse mi4/dense* refers to "arrangement". Hence, they are the cases in which prosodic principle overwhelms Pollyanna Principle.

Then, how about the cases in (B2)? Are they expressing the neutral meanings or referring to the certain characters? The answer is, in most of the contexts, these words are used as the neutral meanings of related properties. Such as 余缺 *yu2/surplus que1/be_short_of* refers to “balance”, 得失 *de2/get shi1/lose* to “result”, 盛衰 *sheng4/prosperity shuai1/decline* to “a life circle”. And, some of them are used as the name of the properties. Such as 厚薄 *hou4/thick bao2/thin* is for the property of “thickness”, 智愚 *zhi4/wise yv2/foolish* for “wisdom” and 大小 *da4/big xiao3/small* for “size”. These evidences support that the compounds in (B2) are not partially-directed compounds.

As to (A5), the lexicalization of 难易 *nan2/difficult yi4/easy* and 轻重 *qing1/light zhong4/heavy* are remained unexplained. As to the concept of a certain property, it is usually to have the positive one in front, like 胖瘦 *pang4/fat shou4/slim*, for “fitness”, 长短 *chang1/long duan3/short*, for “length”, 高低 *gao1/high di1/low*, for “height”, even if this order is against prosodic principle, such as 厚薄 *hou4/thick bao2/thin*, for “thickness”, and 大小 *da4/big xiao3/small*, for “size”. But for the properties of “difficulty” and “weight”, the orders of 难易 *nan2/difficult yi4/easy* and 轻重 *qing1/light zhong4/heavy* are against both semantic and prosodic principles. The reason, we have to say, is still unknown, at least from this study.

As pointed out by Ding and Huang (2014), which we also agree, for the cases in (C1), the reverse orders of each compound are also found acceptable (they are the ones which agree with Pollyanna Principle and prosodic principle). But the two orders bring different readings.

In the lexicon, *si3sheng1* and *sheng1si3*are both loaded. For *si3sheng1*, there are examples like:

(50) 死生有命,富贵在天 (《论语》)

si3/death sheng1/living you3/have ming4/fate, fu4/rich gui4/honored zai4/at tian1/sky
“Important things in life are all depend on fate.”

死生 *si3sheng1* is refer to a life circle (and the things that may happen during the period) and this meaning can be replaced by 生死 *sheng1si3*:

(51) 生死有命,修短素定,非彼药物,所能损益 (《抱朴子》)

sheng1/living si3/death you3/have ming4/fate, xiu1/long duan3/short su4/all ding4/decided, fei1/not bi3/that yao3wu4/medicine, suo3neng2/can sun3/minus yi4/add
“To die or to live, as well as the length of life, are all decided by fate, and that cannot be changed by medicine.”

In some other sentences, 死生 *si3sheng*1 cannot be replaced by 生死 *sheng1si3*:

(52) 死生事大,殡葬改革不可蛮干 (新民晚报)

si3/death sheng1/living shi4/matter da4/important, bin1/funeral zang4/interment gai3ge3/reform bu4/not ke3/can man2/gan4/do "death is an important issue (and therefore) the reform of funeral and interment cannot be rash"

The reform of funeral and interment is about death, not living, hence *si3sheng1* cannot be changed to *sheng1si3*.

When the reading does not particularly refer to death or life, then it is 生死 *sheng1si3* more often chosen than 死生 *si3sheng1*.

(53) 骨癌少年今返医院面对生死 (Google)

gu3/bone ai2/caner shao4nian2/youngster jin1/today fan3/return yi1yuan4/hospital
mian4dui4/face sheng1/living si3/death
"the youngster who has a cancer of bone is returning to hospital today to have a vital treatment"

? 骨癌少年今返医院面对死生

gu3/bone ai2/cancer shao4nian2/youngster jin1/today fan3/return yi1yuan4/hospital
mian4dui4/face si3/death sheng1/living
"the youngster who has a cancer of bone is returning to hospital today to have a vital treatment"

In the situations when both results (to live or to die) are possible, it is normal to have "living" in front of "death".

Hence, there are two usages for *si3sheng1*, one is referring to "a life circle" or to prefer the result of being alive, which can be replaced with *sheng1si3*, and the other one is referring to "death", which cannot be replaced by *sheng1si3*.

For the combination of *si3* and *huo2*, *si3huo2* is the only accepted one. It may mean "the state of being alive or dead" or simply "the state of death". For example:

(54) 他失踪三天了,到现在还不知死活. (Google)

ta1/he shi1zong1/lost san1/three tian1/day le0/LE, dao3/until xian4zai4/now hai2/still
bu4/not zhi1/know si3/death huo2/living
"He has been lost for three days and no trace has been found yet."

The situation of the missing person is unknown, although he probably is dead. In other words, the actually meaning suggests a bad result (death).

It is very interesting to notice the humor in saying 你死我活 *ni3/you si3/death wo3/I huo2/living*:

(55) 拼个你死我活

pin1/fight ge4/CL ni3/you si3/death wo3/I huo2/living
"to have a life or death fight"
* 拼个你活我死
pin1/fight ge4/CL ni3/you huo2/living wo3/I si3/death

"to have a life or death fight"
* 拼个我死你活
pin1/fight ge4/CL wo3/I si3/death ni3/you huo2/living
"to have a life or death fight"
* 拼个我活你死
pin1/fight ge4/CL wo3/I huo2/living ni3/you si3/death
"to have a life or death fight"

The compound *ni3si3wo3huo2* is combined by two opposite pairings, *ni3/you wo3/me* and *si3/death huo2/living*. The meaning of *ni3si3* ("you are dead") equals to that of *wo3huo2* ("I am alive"), which together doubly emphasize the expected result of speaker ("I"). Additionally, for the two pairings, *ni3wo3* and *si3huo2* are the most accepted compound orders, so *wo3huo2ni3si3* is not accepted, even if it may represent the same meaning as *ni3si3wo3huo2*.

Both *chang2duan3* and *duan3chang2* are loaded in Sinica lexicon. But *chang2duan3* is more often used as length, which cannot be replaced by *duan3chang2*, like:

(56) 桌腿长短不一

zhuo1/table tui3/leg chang2/long duan3/short bu4/not yi1/same
"the lengths of table legs are not the same"
*桌腿短长不一
zhuo1/table tui3/leg duan3/short chang2/long bu4/not yi1/same
"the lengths of table legs are not the same"

In contrast, in context with *duan3chang2*, the meaning of *duan3* is more emphasized, like:

(57) 万一他有个短长,一家人都会伤心.

wan4yi1/just_in_case ta1/he you3/have ge4/CL duan3/short chang2/long, yi1/one
jia1/family ren2/people dou1/all hui3/will shang1xin1/sad
"If anything happened to him, the whole family will be sad."
不要在背后论人短长
bu2yao4/not zai4/at bei4hou4/behind lun4/discuss ren2/people duan3/short chang2/long
"Do not judge people secretly."

Duan3chang2 in first sentence refers to some unfortunate issues and in second sentence to the shortage (of someone). They are both partially directed to the metaphor meaning of *duan3*.

Huo4fu2 comes from *Laozi*, a Taoist classic:

(58) 祸兮福所倚,福兮祸所伏.《老子》➔祸福

huo4/unfortunate xi1/XI fu2/fortunate suo3/at yi3/depend, fu2/fortunate xi1/XI
huo4/unfortunate suo3/at fu2/hide
"Unfortunate and fortunate are alternating."

And it therefore generally refers to the meaning of fortunate and unfortunate issues, but partially suggests or emphasizes the unfortunate possibilities:

(59) 天有不测风云,人有旦夕祸福.(元杂剧)

tian1/sky you3/have bu2ce4/unexpected feng1yun2/wind yun2/cloud, ren2/people you3/have dan4/morning xi1/evening huo3/unfortunate fu2/fortunate
"The changing of fate is hard to forecast, just like the changing of weather."

旦夕祸福 *dan4xi1huo4fu2* here has an equal meaning to that of 不测风云 *bu2ce3feng1yun1*. The unexpected wind and cloud is a metaphor of the incidents (祸 *huo4/unfortunate*) in life.

As we can see that, for the partially-directed compounds, in (B2) and (C1), the meanings of the compounds are decided by the native ones, which are placed in the first position. Meanwhile, with the need to complete a bi-syllabic compound, an added word has to be chosen. The added word has to be in the same semantic field as the one with the core meaning. That is to say, the additional word has to have a close semantic relation with the first one. In the end, it is usually the positive pairing member selected, because of the (unconscious) needing of mentioning the bright side of things, which, again, follows the Pollyanna Principle.

The existence of (C2) 浊清 *zhuo2/unclear qing1/clear* is not clear. In fact, 清浊 *qing1/clear zhuo2/unclear* is also accepted in many contexts. It is not found in the lexicon of this study but more common in open resources like Google or Baidu than 浊清 *zhuo2/unclear qing1/clear*. They are used to describe the water (sometimes also the society). We may say that the lack of 清浊 *qing1/clear zhuo2/unclear* is a proof that the lexicon is not complete to cover all the compounds in Chinese.

In sum, the word order of bi-syllabic opposite compounds is decided by semantic principles (Pollyanna Principle, partially-directed compound and temporal order) and prosodic principle. When the two disagree with each other, it is usually semantic principles win out.

Above discussion explains the order of opposite pairing members in the [A][−A] pattern. Next, we move to the other constructions with opposite pairings.

From [A][−A] to Others

In general, the variation of the [A][−A] pattern; that is, the rest of the patterns in category One, the second basic pattern, and the fourth basic pattern, usually follow the order of their according [A][−A] compounds. For example:

(60) 高低 *gao1/high di1/low* ([A][−A])

➔高高低低 *gao1/high gao1/high di1/low di1/low*
*低低高高 *di1/low di1/lowgao1/high gao1/high* ([A][A][−A][−A])
"highs and lows"

(61) 彼此 *bi3/there ci3/here* ([A][−A])

➔彼此彼此 *bi3/there ci3/here bi3/there ci3/here*
*此彼此彼 *ci3/herebi3/there ci3/here bi3/there* ([A][−A][A][−A])
"same here'"

(62) 里外 *li3/inside wai4/outside* ([A][−A])

➔里外里 *li3/inside wai4/outside li3/inside*
*外里外 *wai4/outside li3/insidewai4/outside* ([A][−A][A])
"the whole one"

(63) 是非 *shi4/right fei1/wrong* ([A][−A])

➔是非观 *shi4/right fei1/wrong guan1/principle*
*非是观 *fei1/wrong shi4/right guan1/principle* ([A][−A][X])
"the principle of what is right and what is wrong"

(64) 输赢 *shu1/lose ying2/win* ([A][−A])

➔争输赢 *zheng1/fight_for shu1/lose ying2/win*
*争输赢 *zheng1/fight_for ying2/winshu1/lose* ([X][A][−A])
"to fight for winning the game"

(65) 起落 *qi3/increase luo4/decrease* ([A][−A])

➔大起大落 *da4/extremely qi3/increase da4/extremely luo4/decrease*
*大落大起 *da4/extremely luo4/decreaseda4/extremely qi3/increase*
([S][A][S][−A])
"major ups and downs"

(66) 东西 *dong1/east wai4/west* ([A][−A])

➔东奔西跑 *dong1/east ben1/run xi1/west pao3/run*
*西奔东跑 *xi1/west ben1/run dong1/east pao3/run* ([A][S][−A][S"])
"travelling around"

Sometimes, however, the patterns of [X−][A][+X][−A], [A][X][−A] and [A][X−][−A][+X], are not limited by the [A][−A] compounds with the same pairings. In some cases, both orders work:

(67) 上下 *shang4/up xia4/down* ([A][−A])

➔自上而下 *zi4/from shang4/up er2/to xia4/down* "from up to down"
自下而上 *zi4/from xia4/down er2/to shang4/up* "from down to up"
([X−][A][+X][−A])

(68) 中外 *zhong1/China wai4/abroad* ([A][−A])

➔?中为外用 *zhong1/China wei2/for wai4/abroad yong4/use*
外为中用 *wai4/abroad wei2/for zhong1/China yong4/use* ([A][X−][−A][+X])
"to develop China by using the experience and technology from abroad"

In these examples, the positions of opposite pairing members can be exchanged. And the meanings of the compounds with different orders are also different. In other words, the two compounds have separated but both acceptable meanings. Therefore, they would be used in different contexts. There is no competition between the two compounds. And that is why both orders may be employed in such patterns.

At the same time, in some cases, compounds of these patterns even violate the preferred order:

(69) 是非 *shi4/right fei1/wrong* ([A][−A])

➔*习是成非 *xi2/accustomed shi4/right cheng2/become fei1/wrong*
习非成是 *xi2/accustomed fei1/wrong cheng2/become shi4/right* ([X−][A][+X][−A])
"an accustomed wrong becomes a right one"

(70) 悲喜 *bei1/sad xi3/happy* ([A][−A])

➔*悲极生乐 *bei1/sad ji2/extreme sheng1/become le4/happy*
乐极生悲 *lei4/happy ji2/extreme sheng1/become bei1/sad* ([A][X][−A])
"misery succeeds extreme happiness"

(71) 好坏 *hao3/good huai4/bad* ([A][−A])

➔*泰极否来 *tai4/fortunate ji2/extreme pi3/unfortunate lai2/come*
否极泰来 *pi3/unfortunate ji2/extreme tai4/fortunate lai2/come* ([A][X−][−A][+X])
"when situation cannot be worse, there comes the turning point"

In these examples, it is the order against which the initial one is accepted. That, again, is explained by the meaning of whole structure. 习非成是 *xi2fei1cheng2shi4* is used to describe the situation that an accustomed wrong is generally treated as a right one; but the reverse order of *shi4/right* and *fei2/wrong* makes the meaning of "an accustomed right becoming a wrong one", which would not happen in the real world and therefore cannot be accepted in language. 乐极生悲 *le4ji2sheng1bei1* and 否极泰来 *pi3ji2tai4lai2* have in common the meaning of "goodness and badness always follow each in extreme situations", and both of the orders in these two compounds are fixed. Like 自上而下 *zi4shang4er2xia4* and 自下而上 *zi4xia4er2shang4*, they are complementary in semantic meaning and therefore do not have competition in context. But since the compound of 乐极生悲 *le4ji2sheng1bei1* is lexicalized, and the opposite meaning is satisfied by 否极泰来 *pi3ji2tai4lai2*; therefore, *悲极生乐 *bei1ji2sheng1le4* is not acceptable. Neither do the compound of *泰极否来 *tai4ji2pi3lai2*. Hence, in the patterns of [X−][A][+X][−A], [A][X][−A] and [A][X−][−A][+X], the order of opposite pairing members is decided by the semantic meaning of the structure.

For the third basic pattern; that is, the compounds having two pairs of opposites within one compound or idiom, the ordering rules are generalized as follow (Ding and Huang 2014: 14–15):

1. The positive one(s) is/are preferred to take the prior place(s).
   There are only three possible orderings in our corpus, and within them: [P(ostive)1][N(egative)1][P(ositive)2][N(egative)2] > [P1][N1][N2][P2] (安危祸福 *an1/safe wei1/dangerous huo4/unfortunate fu2/fortunate*, 是非曲直 *shi4/right fei1/wrong qu3/bend zhi2/straight*, 是非黑白 *shi4/right fei1/wrong hei1/black bai2/white*) > [N1][P1][N2][P2] (悲欢离合 *bei1/sad huan1/happy li2/apart he2/together*, 轻重缓急 *qing1/light zhong4/heavy huan3/slow ji2/hurry*).
   That is to say, [P1][N1][P2][N2] is the most common order.
2. The words sharing the same natural domain are preferred to appear in close positions. Hence, 男女老少 *nan2/male nv3/female* (both for gender) *lao3/old shao4/young* (both for age), "all the people", is preferred over男老少女 *nan2/male lao3/old shao4/young nv3/female* or 男老女少 *nan2/male lao3/old nv3/female shao4/young* (this compound may be possible when it means "the male one is older and the female one is younger", which differs from the meaning of *nan2nv3lao3shao4*). And, 亲疏远近 *qin1/close shu1/remote* (both for relationship) *yuan3/distant jin4/close* (both for distance), "close and distant", rather than 亲远近疏 *qin1/close yuan3/distant jin4/close shu1/remote*; 利弊得失 *li4/advantage bi4/disadvantage* ("cons and pros") *de2/win shi1/lose* (both for the possible results), "all the aspects", rather than 利失得弊 *li4/advantage shi1/lose de2/win bi4/disadvantage*.
3. If the same domain has more than one way of being divided, then the ones which share the same dividing way should be placed together. For example, 前后左右, *qian2/front* with *hou3/behind*, and *zuo3/left* with *you4/right*. And, 加减乘除, *jia1/addition* with *jian3/subtraction*, and *cheng2/multiplication* with *chu2/division*, according to the rules of arithmetic operation.

From the aspect of opposite sub-category, different kinds of opposites perform differently with the rules. For antonym and complementary compounds, it is true that most of the instances prefer to have the positive ones in front: 亲疏 *qin1/close shu1/distant* 优劣 *you1/good(_quantity)lie4/bad(_quantity)* 利害 *li4/benefit hai4/harm* 善恶 *shan4/kindhearted e4/evil* 多寡 *duo1/manygua3/few* 尊卑 *zun1/respected bei1/humble*.

For taxonomy words, there are many compounds like文武 *wen2/civil wu3/military* 经纬 *jing1/horizontalwei3/latitudinal* 水火 *shui3/water huo3/fire* 南北 *nan2/south bei3/north*, that it is hard to evaluate the polarity. In other words, the hypothesis is not applicable to these examples. Some taxonomy compounds, such as甘苦 *gan1/sweet ku3/bitter* 爱恨 *ai4/love hen4/hate*, have the culturally positive words in front. But, it also has compounds like 悲喜 *bei1/sad xi3/happy* or 阴阳 *yin1/Yinyang2/Yang*, which have the culturally negative ones in front. From the examples of taxonomy group, Ding and Huang (2014: 16) add some rules to Tang's list:

(16) "古" > "今" (the concept of *gu3* "ancient" prior to that of *jin1* "nowadays")
(17) "东" > "西" (the concept of *dong1* "east" prior to that of *xi1* "west")
(18) "南" > "北" (the concept of *nan2* "south" prior to that of *bei3* "north")
(19) "经" > "纬" (the concept of *jing1* "horizontal" prior to that of *wei3* "latitudinal")
(20) "昼" > "夜" (the concept of *zhou4* "day" prior to that of *ye4* "night").
(21) "头" > "尾" (the concept of *tou2* "head" prior to that of *wei3* "end")
(22) "左" > "右" (the concept of *zuo3* "left" prior to that of *you4* "right")
(23) "前" > "后" (the concept of *qian2* "front" prior to that of *hou4* "behind")
(24) "天" > "地" (the concept of *tian1* "sky" prior to that of *di4* "earth").

3.5 Summary

In this chapter, we extract the constructions containing at least one opposite pairing from a lexicon of bi-syllable to quad-syllable. Result shows there are four basic patterns: (1) the ones containing only one opposite pairing; (2) the ones containing one opposite pairing with linking word(s); (3) the ones containing two opposite pairings; (4) the ones containing one opposite pairing with one synonym pairing.

The meaning of each pattern is decided by the construction itself (such as [A] [−A]) and the linking word(s) (such as *from... to...*). The semantic functions of these patterns can be divided along a logic standard: to cover every member of the whole scale; to emphasize the middle of the scale, and/or to negate or ignore the two extreme points; to emphasize the two extreme points of the scale, and to negate or ignore the middle of the scale; or to emphasize one of the two extreme points and negate the other one; scale changing; under specialized; or others, like, eventual expressions.

Within the constructions, the order of opposite pairing members is decided by a combination of several principles. For antonym and complementary pairs, Pollyanna Principle and prosodic principle together determine the order; while for converse pairs, temporal order is the crucial principle. The discussion also shows that Pollyanna Principle has its limitation on Chinese data.

Chapter 4
Opposites in Discourse

4.1 Research Question and Previous Experiments

4.1.1 Research Question

In Chap. 3, we study the constructions from bi-syllable to quad-syllable with (at least) one opposite pairings. In this chapter, we extend the study to a larger scale, that is, discourse, to see how the opposite pairings are used in it.

4.1.2 Previous Experiments

4.1.2.1 Syntactic Frames and Discourse

A Starting Point on English

Based on the realization that a large corpus data should be used in the study of antonyms, Jones (2002) starts his work with a corpus of 280 million words from newspaper texts, dated between 1 Oct. 1988 and 31 Dec. 1996.

Fifty-six antonym pairs are selected by Jones, "largely on my own intuition" (2002: 29) but also referring to Deese's (1964) list and *Roget's Thesaurus* (1952). The new pair list is supposed to exclusively contain the highest frequency English antonymous pairs, which are "gradable, non-morphological, adjectival pairs" (2002: 30). These antonym pairs contribute to a database of 3,000 sentences, by co-occurrence of pair members. Then, the sentences are categorized according to their discourse functions.[1]

[1]The term "discourse function" in this thesis is following the same term used in Jones (2002) and their later works. It is not the same reading as it has in discourse analysis.

J. Ding, *A Lexical Semantic Study of Chinese Opposites*,
Frontiers in Chinese Linguistics 1, https://doi.org/10.1007/978-981-10-6184-4_4

Jones observes that, for most of the antonym pairs in the database, there are two "major" functions; that is, Ancillary Antonymy (which accounted for 38.7%) and Coordinated Antonymy (which accounted for 38.4%).

Examples for **Ancillary Antonymy** include:

(a) As the Governor of Kumomoto province told me, "This is a ***rich*** *country*, with ***poor*** *people*".
(b) I ***love*** to *cook* but I ***hate*** *doing the dishes*—so I'd have a dishwasher or a family of gypsies to do the washing up.
(c) Since then, of course, they've all had knighthoods, usually when they're too ***old*** to play *Hamlet,* but too ***young*** to play *butlers in Hollywood movies*.

(originally from Jones 2002: 45–6, 5f, 5a, 5c)

In sentence a, the antonym pair of *rich* and *poor* also triggers the contrast between *country* and *people*. In sentence b, the second contrast is found between *cook* and *doing the dishes*, of which the later pairing member is not a word but a phrase. *Hamlet* and *butlers in Hollywood movies* are signaled as opposites because of the setting in the according position with *old* and *young* respectively. In sentence c, Jones notes that it is striking to observe quite a number of sentences with antonym co-occurrences that actually feature more than only one contrast. And sometimes, the contrast of existing antonyms might be emphasized by the other contrast:

(d) If so, unemployment may rise more ***quickly*** *now*, but more ***slowly*** *later*.

(originally from Jones, 2002: 46, 5 h)

For this sentence, there are two antonym pairs—*quickly* and *slowly*, *now* and *later*. The parallel use inspires the interaction of both pairs and results in a much stronger contrast reading.

The other major function of antonym pairing in context is "to signal inclusiveness or exhaustiveness of scale", which is named **Coordinated Antonymy** by Jones, for example:

(a) While pensions will not be abolished, the government will encourage everyone, ***rich*** and ***poor***, to rely for their retirement mainly on money they invest in private pension funds.
(b) Whether he was ***right*** or ***wrong*** to raise a certain matter in the way he did, Mr. Lawson offered an important insight into his, and almost certainly Mrs. Thatcher's and John Moore's, thinking about the long-term future of welfare state.

(originally from Jones, 2002: 61, 22a, 22c)

In sentence a, the antonym pair *rich* and *poor* is used to indicate that personal financial state is not relevant to the statement that everyone should rely on his or her own investment. Sentence b is trying to avoid discussing whether Mr. Lawson is *right* or *wrong* to raise a certain matter but focuses on the fact that he did offer an important insight. Coordinated Antonymy might be triggered by certain frames like

X and Y, *X or Y*, *X as well as Y* and so on. Jones concludes that Ancillary Antonymy, is used to "maximize the contrastive power of antonyms", while Coordinated Antonymy is used to "allow that contrastive power to remain dormant" (2002:74).

Also, there are still a number of "minor" functions of antonym pairs, such as **Comparative Antonymy** (6.8%):

(a) Sometimes I feel more ***masculine*** than ***feminine*** and I don't like it.

(originally from Jones, 2002: 76, 37c)

Comparative Antonymy can be triggered by frames like *more X than Y*, *X is more [adj.] than Y* or *X rather than Y*. It is defined as, "[t]he co-occurrence of an antonymous pair within a framework that places those words in a comparative context or measures one antonym against the other." (2002: 76).

And, **Distinguished Antonymy** (5.4%), with frames which include *the difference between X and Y*, *separating X and Y*, *a gap between X and Y*, and with examples like:

(b) Scientists admit that the discrepancies between ***male*** and ***female*** brains may be less important than education and experience.

(originally from Jones, 2002: 81, 44c)

Distinguished Antonymy's definition is, "[t]he co-occurrence of an antonymous pair within a framework that alludes to the inherent semantic dissimilarity of those words." (2002: 81)

Transitional Antonymies (3.0%) are the ones "with a framework that expresses a movement or change from one location or state to another". Its typical frames include *from X to Y*, *turning X into Y*, *X gives way to Y*, and it triggers examples like:

(c) Inflation is a tax which redistributes wealth to the ***sophisticated*** from the ***unsophisticated***.

(originally from Jones 2002: 86, 51a)

Negated Antonymy (2.1%) is the antonymous pair which "within a framework that negated one antonym as a device to augment the other". (2002: 88). Its typical frames are like *X not Y*, *X instead of Y*, *X as opposed to Y*, with examples like:

(d) The case for treating animals better is so intellectually convincing that ours is not a cause to ***win***, ours is a cause to ***lose***.

(originally from Jones, 2002: 89, 56c)

And some non-standard frameworks like:

(e) It is a challenge which says, ***implicitly*** if not ***explicitly***, that the Fifth Estate itself is a piece of journalistic mythical self-creation the justification of which is questionable in reality.

(originally from Jones, 2002: 90, 58b)

Extreme Antonymy (1.3%), "within a framework that unites the outer-most areas of their given semantic scale" (2002: 91), which has frames like *the very X and the very Y*, *either too X or too Y*, *deeply X and deeply Y*, triggers examples like:

(f) It is often considered a safer and gentler form of treatment, especially valuable to the very ***young*** and the very ***old***, being less toxic and having fewer side effects.

(originally from Jones, 2002: 91, 59a)

The last category is called **Idiomatic Antonymy** (0.8%), for the antonyms in idiomatic expressions. According to Jones, they "would be recognised as a familiar idiom, proverb or cliche". (2002: 93) Examples of this category include:

(g) *Penny wise and pound foolish*
(h) *Easy come, easy go.*
(i) *through thick and thin*

(originally from Jones, 2002: 93)

There are still 106 sentences that remain in Jones's database. The patterns of these sentences are weaker and less frequent than the ones in identified frames. Hence, they are accounted as the residual sentences.

Jones (2006) continues the research of antonym co-occurrence with a corpus of adult spoken English and the results confirmed his findings in 2002, with frequency differences in Ancillary Antonymy (28.8%) and Coordinated Antonymy (31.3%). Similar results were also found in children-produced examples (45.6% for Ancillary Antonymy and 22.9% for Coordinated Antonymy) and child-directed examples (39.1% for Ancillary Antonymy and 18.4% for Coordinated Antonymy) in Murphy and Jones' (2008) work.

Muehleisen and Isono (2009) then extend the researches on antonym discourse functions into Swedish and Japanese, respectively, to see if the discourse functions of antonym co-occurrence are used in languages other than English.

Experiment on Japanese

Muehleisen and Isono (2009) follow the same research method but employed it to Japanese, a language which is much less similar to English.

Given the differences between Japanese and English in terms of "morphology, syntax, orthography and discourse features", the authors decide to choose "some prototypical antonyms", rather than to translate near-equivalents for the English pairing lists in Jones's work. Almost all the twelve words (11 out of 12) are considered as "prototypical or close-to-prototypical antonyms" by the related study on Japanese (Nishio 1972; Cf. Muehleisen and Isono 2009). The 12 pairings (roughly in English are, "shallow-deep", "small-big", "close-far", "old-new", "fat-thin", "wide-narrow", "dark-light", "long-short", "heavy-light", "many-few", "high-low", "strong-weak").

Then, 600 sentences are extracted from a 253 million-word Japanese corpus of the Leeds Collection of Internet Corpora, which is balanced with a wide range of topics of texts from Internet. In these sentences, 54.8% were categorized as Ancillary Antonymy and only 13% as Coordinated Antonymy. The categories included Transitional Antonymy (8.7%), Simultaneous Antonymy (7%), Disjunctive Antonymy (6.2%), Comparative Antonymy (2.5%), Negated Antonymy (2.3%) and Distinguished Antonymy (1%). Only 4.5% of the instances were left in the "Other" category.

Such statistical results are quite dissimilar with that of English or Swedish. However, as claimed by the authors, it again confirms that the discourse functions of co-occurring antonyms work for languages other than English, but may vary in distribution for different languages.

4.1.2.2 Measurement of Canonicity

As we can see in Sect. 2.2, it is interesting to ask whether there any good opposites, or canonical opposite pairings? And, what are the factors to decide the canonicity of being opposite pairings? With large data, these questions could be answered.

Justeson and Katz (1991) point out that the distinction between being antonymous and not, might not be dichotomous, but "may be more or less antonymous" (1991: 147). Jones et al. (2007) use lexico-grammatical constructions to measure the canonicity of antonym pairings. By using the World Wide Web as a corpus, they set up experiments based on constructions in which antonym pairings are expected to co-occur much more frequently than the average rate. Fourteen contrastive constructions, such as X and Y alike, between X and Y, both X and Y, either X or Y, from X to Y, X versus Y and whether X or Y, are built to tackle antonym co-occurrence in discourse.

These grammatical constructions are known with a significantly high frequency of antonym pairings. Hence, the constructions are tracing words in either X or Y position.

Jones et al. conclude that the methodology they use for indicating the canonicity of antonym pairings was "highly appropriate". Moreover, the paper claims to support the finding that co-occurrence is both a cause of antonymy (as founded by Charles and Miller 1989) and as "a key symptom" to "gauge the strength of the antonym relation". And, "repeated co-occurrence across a wide range of antonyms frames is a better indicator of canonicity than either raw frequency counting or metalinguistic experimentation" (2007: 150–1).

Paradis et al. (2009) use a psycholinguistic experiment and theirs final results indicate that: first, non-canonical antonym reaction times are found to be affected by "the semantic divergence between the members of the pair" (Charles et al. 1994; Cf. Paradis et al. 2009: 384), which means the farther one antonym candidate lies from the given word, the longer time subjects would need to react to it; second, "canonical antonyms have been found to prime each other more strongly than non-canonical opposites (Becker, 1980)" (2009: 384).

The results of Paradis et al.'s (2009) elicitation experiment suggests—and as also confirmed by similar results in Jones et al.'s (2007) web study—that there is a scale of canonicity from the perfect antonym candidate to the "no preferred partners" or "not-so-good ones". For some words, their antonym members are very easily defined and elicited in test as the same ones by different language users, while for some other words, the answers vary to different persons or in different contexts.

Jones et al. (2012) summarized the series of work on antonym canonicity into the following points:

1. "There is a dichotomy between good and bad antonyms", since there are obvious differences between the judgment experiment and elicitation experiment;
2. For the group of non-canonical antonyms, there is a continuum of the canonicity curve, which is supported by the judgment experiment and the web-as-corpus study;
3. "Canonicity is a gradable property" and antonyms are a conceptual relation (2012: 70).

4.2 Methodology, Candidate List and Corpus

4.2.1 Methodology

Our Chinese experiment was separated into four steps:

Step 1: using the **candidate pairings** in a **sample corpus** for **collocation**;
Step 2: generalizing **syntactic frames** from these collocated sentences;
Step 3: with the syntactic frames (from Step 2) and candidate pairings (from Step 1) to extract sentences from a **main corpus**;
Step 4: classifying the extracted sentences (from Step 3) into different **discourse functions** and analyzing the result.

Why do we repeat the experiment in two corpora? Since Chinese is a language different from English in many aspects, the design—especially the syntactic frames—used for English cannot be used in Chinese directly. Hence, it is necessary to modify the original methodology in Chinese experiment. Then, how to have the applicable syntactic frames? We design a sample experiment to extract the syntactic frames and apply them in a later main experiment (Fig. 4.1).

Fig. 4.1 Flowchart of Chinese experiment on opposites in discourse

4.2.2 *Problems in Chinese Experiment*

By employing the same approach from English to Japanese, Muehleisen and Isono (2009) find that characteristics of Japanese antonyms influenced the results of the Japanese experiment. Similar to that of Japanese, Chinese also has its own characteristics, which may cause problems for our experiment.

Segmentation

The first problem is caused by the writing system of Chinese. For languages like English, each word separates from others with a space in between. However, because Chinese is written in characters, the segmentation between each character does not necessarily represent the stop between words. For example:

(72) 好的品质 hao3/good de0/DE ping3zhi4/quality “good qualities”
(73) 好心人 hao3/good xin1/hear ren2/people “people with a warm heart”
(74) 好看 hao3/good kan4/looking “good looking”

Hao3 in example (72) is an individual adjective for *pin3zhi4*; in example (73), it is used with *xin1* as one word meaning “kind/kindness”; in example (74), *hao3kan4* is one word. Besides, *hao3* in example (72) is usually used as an opposite of *huai4/bad*, while *hao3kan4* is opposite to *nan2kan4/ugly*. Hence, we can see that, segmentation is a crucial information in the Chinese experiment.

Part of Speech
Then, for the same character in Chinese, its word class (part of speech, POS) may change with contexts.

(75) 肥: 瘦 *fei2/fat: shou4/slim*:

肥了地方, 瘦了国家
fei1/fat le/LE di4fang1/region, shou4/slim le/LE guo2jia1/nation
“the regional government is becoming richer while the national government is becoming poorer”

In example (75), *fei2* and *shou4* usually use as adjectives for modifying someone or something sharp, but here they are used as verbs, meaning “becoming richer (fatter) or poorer (slimmer)”, as one does with a metaphor. The characters do not change but the grammatical functions they have are different.

(76) 开放: 封闭*kai1fang4/open: feng1bi4/closed*:

开放的风气 *kai1fang4/open de/DE feng1qi4/style* “open manner”
封闭的思想 *feng1bi4/closed de/DE si1xiang3/mind* “fossil mind”
开门与关窗 *kai1/open men2/door yu3/and guan1/close chuan1/window* “to open the window and close the door”

In example (76), *kai1fang4* and *kai1* are both under the conceptual group of *kai1/open*. *Kai1fang4* can be used as an adjective to modify *feng1qi4*, while *kai1* is used as a verb for “to open” or “opening” in *kai1men2*. Similarly, *feng1bi4* is used as an adjective for *si1xiang3* while *guan1* as a verb in “to close the window”, although the two words are both found in the same concept of *guan1/close*.

(77) 冷: 热 *leng3/cold: re4/hot*:

战酷暑,斗严寒
zhan4/fight ku4/extreme shu3/hotness, dou4/struggle yan2/severely han2/coldness
“to struggle with formidable weather conditions, like scorching summer and freezing winter”
身上很冷
shen1/body shang4/on hen3/very leng3/cold
“the body is cold”
天冷下来了

tian1/weather leng3/cold xia4lai2/down le/LE
"the weather is becoming cold"

In example (77), *ku4shu3* is a noun for the concept of *hot/hotness* and *yan2han2* is a noun for that of cold/coldness. And, *leng3* is used as adjective in sentence 2. In sentence 3, *leng3* is used as verb for "becoming cold".

Hence, in our experiment, we do not restrict the part of speech of candidate words in extraction. However, in one sentence, A and –A should be the same POS. Theoretical studies agree that the grammatical functions of opposite pairing members are the same (e.g., Zhang 1979; He et al. 1983). In our practical study, this restriction is specially designed to avoid the false examples caused by polysemous candidates. For instance, 次(*ci4*) is listed by *Tongyici Cilin*as a synonym of 坏 (huai4, "*bad"*). Meanwhile, 次 in Chinese is also used as a highly frequent measure word. It is hard to say which meaning is more basic for 次. However, in the test experiment, majority of the extracted sentences are using 次 as the measure word. There are many false examples like:

(78) 第一次见到质量这样好的绒

di4yi1/first ci4/measure_word jian4dao4/see zhi4liang4/qulity zhe4yang4/this
hao3/good de0/DE rong2/cashmere
"it is the first time to see such a good cashmere"

(79) 一次好远好远的航行

yi1/one ci4/measure_wordhao4/very yuan4/distant hao2/very yuan3/distant de0/DE
hang2xing2/voyage
"a very long voyage"

That naturally results in the obviously low accuracy of the data for次*ci4*. For that reason, we insist that the POS of two pairing words in the same context, have to be the same. It increases the accuracy of examples with polysemous words like 次*ci4*.

Word Length

Previous studies have had rough discussion on whether the opposite pairing members should have the same character numbers. In other words, is it appropriate to name monosyllable word 瘦*shou4/thin* and bi-syllabic word 肥胖 *fei2pang4/fat*, or even, phrase like 臃肿不堪 *yong1zhong3bu4kan1/fat*, as opposite pairings?

Zhou (1985) points out that opposite relations can be built between different grammatical levels, such as word to word, word to phrase, fixed phrase to fixed phrase, or, phrase to phrase. Qian (1982) argues that the construction of pairing members must be the same. But Wu and Wang (1983), Shi and Zhan (1983) all do not agree on this point.

Hence, which theoretical point is preferred by native users has not been recovered by real language data yet. So in our experiment, we do not restrict the character number of pairing members to be the same, in order to see if the words or phrases having the same characters would be more easily to combine a pair. That is to say, co-occurrence of 便宜 *pian2yi4/cheap* and 贵 *gui4/expensive* can be extracted by our patterns. We relaxed the restriction to test whether the conclusions in previous studies also apply to opposite pairings, by looking at the syllable numbers of pairings. And that is one of the main points which will be described in our summary for the experiment.

4.2.3 Candidate List and Corpus

Candidate List

This work is not going to exhaust all the Chinese concepts. We select 22 opposite concept pairs which are very common in Chinese. In the list there are 5 complementary concept pairs, 12 antonym concept pairs, and 5 converse concept pairs. The listed pairs should be the ones either mentioned in previous studies (for the comparison among Chinese and other languages) or have many synonyms (for the measurement of canonicity).

Complementary pairings are not very easy to find in natural language usage. Theoretical discussions of opposite categorization agree that complementary opposites are not gradable. Complementary opposite pairings are considered to di-chometic to the domain they are applied, and therefore do not allow the existence of an in-between area. However, in real everyday language use, it is hard to find such pairings that cannot be gradual in any case. Even for the pairing of *alive: dead*, it is common to have the sayings such as "she is half-dead from hunger", or, "somebody is more dead than alive". Neither of the two subjects of these examples is actually dead but the sayings reflect the fact that when we are using languages, theoretical di-chometic is not always applicable. Therefore it results in the difficulty of finding "real" complementary pairings.

The five concepts pairs below are the ones we considered to be the most common complementary pairings in Chinese. Some of them, like 生:死 (*sheng1/alive: si3/dead*) and 男:女 (*nan2/male: nv3/female*), have been discussed in earlier studies for a long time (Lyons 1968; Cruse 1986; Croft and Cruse 2004, among others). The others are not so popular among theorists, but are also cited as the typical pair members under the complementary categorization. Hence, they are supposed to inspire minimal argument when being called "complementary (opposites)" (Table 4.1).

In our experiment, the result of antonyms is going to be compared with the ones of English and Japanese. So, the ones used in their studies should be included in our list. They are: *fast: slow*, *bright: dull*, *strong: weak*, *big: small*, *wide: narrow*, *good: bad* and *thick: thin*. Some of the pairs in previous studies, such as *shallow: deep*, *close: far* and *many: few*, do not have many synonyms in our data resource (*Tongyici Cilin* 2005, see the next section for details), and it would have negative influence on the later measurement for canonicity. So we do not include them in the list. Besides, we add five new pairs for the category of antonym. They are 冷: 热

Table 4.1 5 complementary concept pairs for Chinese experiment in discourse

生:死;	男:女;	真:假;	开:合;	奇:偶
sheng1: si3;	*nan2: nv3*;	*zhen1: jia3*;	*kai1: he2*;	*ji1: ou3*
alive: dead;	male: female;	true: false;	open: close;	odd: even

Table 4.2 12 antonym concept pairs for Chinese experiment in discourse

快:慢;	明:暗;	强:弱;	大:小;	宽:窄;	好:坏;
kuai4: man4;	*ming2: an4*;	*qiang2: ruo4*;	*da4: xiao3*;	*kuan1: zhai3*;	*hao3: huai4*
fast: slow;	bright: dark;	strong: weak;	big: small;	wide: narrow;	good: bad;
厚:薄;	冷:热;	贵:贱;	肥:瘦;	美:丑;	智:愚
hou4: bo2	*leng3: re4*;	*gui4: jian4*;	*fei2: shou4*;	*mei3: chou3*;	*zhi4: yu2*
thick: thin;	cold: hot;	expensive: cheap;	fat: slim;	beautiful: ugly;	clever: foolish

Table 4.3 5 converse concept pairs for Chinese experiment in discourse

买:卖;	教:学;	来:去;	取:舍;	施:受
Mai3: mai4;	*jiao1: xue2*;	*lai2: qu4*;	*qu3: she3*;	*shi1: shou4*
Buy: sell;	teach: learn;	come: go;	take: offer;	give: receive

(*leng3/cold: re4/hot*); 贵:贱 (*gui4/expensive: jian4/cheap*); 肥:瘦 (*fei2/fat: shou4/slim*); 美:丑 (*mei3/beautiful: chou3/ugly*); 智:愚 (*zhi4/clever: yu2/foolish*). These concepts have large numbers of synonyms in *Tongyici Cilin* (Table 4.2).

The five converse pairs we have are the typical ones in this category (Table 4.3).

We refer to *Tongyici Cilin* (extended version) (HIT-SCIR, 2005) for the candidate list of opposite conceptual pairs. This dictionary is organized by synonym and/or near-synonym relations. The first version (Mei et al. 1983) contains 53,859 entries. But many of the entries are no longer used today. Based on the paper version of *Tongyici Cilin* (1983), Research Center for Social Computing and Information Retrieval, Harbin Institute of Technology (HIT-SCIR) removes the entries occurring less than 3 times in People's Daily Corpus, reducing the size to 39,099. Then HIT-SCIR uses existing electronic dictionaries to add more recent entries to generate a new lexicon of 77,343 entries. The entries are grouped by their lexical-semantic relationship and the ones with similar or close meanings are organized under the same community. The electronic version of this resource is considered to be the most completed one for synonyms and is widely employed by researchers in Natural Language Processing area for Chinese.

In *Tongyici Cilin*, the concepts of 冷 *leng3/cold* and 热*re4/hot* are listed as (Fig. 4.2):

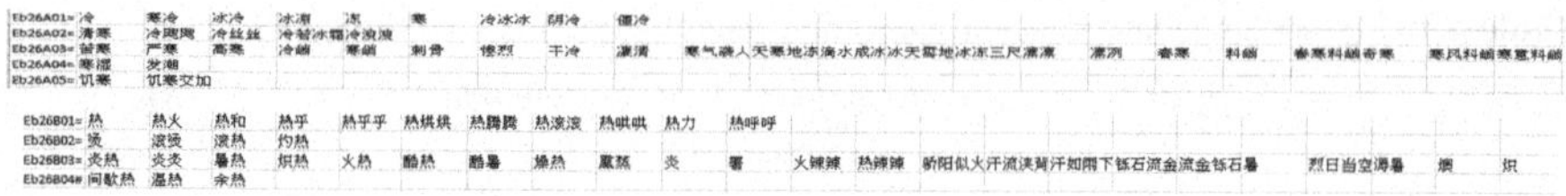

Fig. 4.2 Synonym lists of *leng3/cold* and *re4/hot* in *Tongyici Cilin*

Eb26A is for the concept of *cold*, with Eb26B is for the one of *hot*, and their synonyms are listed as the sub-groups.

Not all the synonyms in *Tongyici Cilin* are used in our experiment. Some words are removed from the candidate list for different reasons. For example, 大 *da4* in the conceptual group of "expensive" is taken out because the basic meaning of *da4* is "big" rather than "expensive". If not, the co-occurrence of *da4* and words of "cheap" group would contribute a lot of false sentences, like:

(80) 每年都有**大**批反季节蔬菜运往北国的海南岛,今年有些品种菜**贱**伤农.

mei3/every nian2/year dou1/all you3/have da4/big pi1/amount fan3/anti-ji4jie2/season shu1cai4/vegetable yun4/travel wang3/to bei3guo2/north de0/DE hai3nan2/Hainan dao3/island, jin1/this nian2/year you3xie1/some pin1zhong3/kind cai4/vetegable jian4/cheap shang1/hurt nong2/farmer
"Every year, there is a lot of anti-season vegetable travelling to Hainan; this year, some kinds of them are too cheap to cover the cost of farmers."

In the above example, the word 大 *da4/big* is used to modify the quantity of vegetable and does not have the meaning of being expensive. Hence this sentence is not valid.

Apart from this, the dialect words and words which are not very common in modern Mandarin were also moved out from the list, like 燠 *yu4/hot*.

Words like 发潮 *fa1chao2* "being wet" in "cold" group actually do not have the meaning of "being cold". Such words should be removed.

Some words occur in both sides of the two concept pairs and they should be moved out. For example, 换 *huan4/exchange* represents the movement of goods or money from one side to another side, as we can say:

(81) 拿钱**换**东西

na2/use qian2/money huan4/exchange dong1xi1/issue
"using money to buy things"

(82) 卖东西**换**钱

mai4/sell dong1xi1/issue huan4/exchange qian2/money
"selling things to earn money"

So the character of *huan4* is found in both the groups of *mai3/buy* and *mai4/sell*. To include *huan4* would reduce the accuracy of the data results; therefore such words are taken out from the candidate list.

A full list of candidate words can be found in Appendix B.

Corpus: Chinese GigaWord Corpus (2005)

Chinese GigaWord Simplified Corpus (henceforth GigaWord or GigaWord Corpus) was chosen because it is very large in size and offers high quality segmentation and POS labelling.

GigaWord Corpus is the largest tagged corpus for modern simplified Chinese and contains 250,124,230 tokens from China's Xinhua News Agency (Mainland), Central News Agency (Taiwan), and Zaobao Newspaper (Singapore), from middle 90s to middle 00s. The significant size of this corpus is good enough to fulfill our research need. Besides, as described in Huang et al. (1997), all the texts are automatically segmented and POS-tagged with the Academia Sinica segmentation and tagging system, and then partially post-checked by humans. The final accuracy of the 250 million tokens reaches around 95% (Ma and Huang 2006). The high accuracy of segmentation is extremely important for our Chinese experiment. And that is also the reason why we do not run the experiment in open online resources like Google or Baidu.

Another reason to choose GigaWord Corpus is that, the one for English study is also a corpus from newspaper texts. The 280 million words in Jones's corpus come from papers of *The Independent*, from Oct 1st, 1988 to Dec 31st, 1996. The 253 million-word Japanese corpus is a part of the Leeds Collection of Internet Corpora. It is also a balanced corpus. Such similarity in size, date (all for modern writing) and genre gives us the assurance that the result of our Chinese experiment is comparable to these of other languages.

In Step 1 of our experiment, we choose Sinica Corpus as the sample corpus. Sinica Corpus is one part of the GigaWord Corpus so the segmentation and POS information generalized from sample test may be inherited by GigaWord, in Step 3.

Syntactic Frames

We translated the frames from Jones's categorization (2002) to Chinese ones:

Our sample experiment offers more syntactic frames for Chinese. Ancillary Antonymy does not have certain frames but it is supposed to be constructed by two contrasts, so in Chinese sentences like 政治冷*zheng4zhi4/politics leng3/cold* "being frigid in politics", 经济热*jing1ji4/economy re4/hot* "being close in economy" would be classified in this category, and such syntactic frames are generalized as "noun X, noun Y" (Table 4.4).

Additionally, we learn some new syntactic frames from these sentences, extracted in the sample test. For example, Distinguished Antonymy can also be realized by syntactic frames like:

(83) 时而X时而Y *shi2er2/sometimes X shi2er2/sometimes Y*

时而高时而低*shi2er2/sometimes gao1/high shi2er2/sometimes di1/low* "sometimes high sometimes low"

(84) 若X若Y *rou4/like X rou4/like* Y

若明若暗*rou4/like ming2/bright rou4/like an4/dark* "hazy"

Table 4.4 Chinese translation of english syntactic frames used in Jones (2002)

Jone's (2002) Classes[a]	English syntactic frames	Chinese translation
Coordinated antonymy	Both X and Y Either X or Y Neither X or Y X and Y alike X as well as Y Whether X or Y	X和 Y X 或者Y 既不是X也不是Y X 和 Y 相同 X 以及 Y 要么X 要么Y
Comparative antonymy	More X than Y X is more [adj.] than Y X rather than Y	比Y 更X X 比 Y 更…… 是 X 而不是 Y
Distinguished antonymy	The difference between X and Y Separating X and Y A gap between X and Y	X 和 Y 之间的不同 区分 X 和 Y X和Y 之间的鸿沟
Transitional antonymy	From X to Y Turning X to Y X gives ways to Y	从 X 到 Y 从 X 转变为 Y X 让位给 Y
Negated antonymy	X not Y X instead of Y X as opposed to Y	是X 不是 Y X 而不是 Y X 是 Y 的反面
Extreme antonymy	The very X and the very Y Either too X or too Y Deeply X and deeply Y	非常X非常Y 要么太X 要么太Y 极度X 极度Y

[a]Ancillary Antonymy and other minor classes, such as Idiomatic Antonymy, Conflict, Oblique stroke and so on, were not listed in this table since Jones (2002) did not generalize their patterns

(85) 什么是X什么是Y *shen1me0/what shi4/BE X shen1me0/what shi4/BE Y*

他知道什么是聪明的改变，什么是愚蠢的改变
ta1/he zhi1dao4/know shen1me0/what shi4/BE cong1ming1/clever de0/DE gai3bian4/change, shen1me0/what shi4/BE yu2chun3/foolish de0/DE gai2bian4/change
"He know what is a clever change and what is a foolish one."

And, frames for Negated Antonymy include:

(86) 不X反Y *bu2/not X fan3/but Y*

不快反慢*bu2/not kuai4/fast fan3/but man4/slow*
"not hurry up but slow down"

(87) 讴歌X鞭笞Y *ou1ge2/eulogize X bian1chi4/flog Y*

讴歌光明,鞭笞黑暗
ou1ge2/eulogize guang1ming2/brightness bian1chi4/flog hei1an4/darkness
"to eulogize the positive sides and flog the negative sides"

(88) verb X 不verb Y

只传女儿,不传儿子
zhi3/only chuan2/teach nv3er0/daughter, bu4/not chuan2/teach er2zi0/son
"(this skill) being only taught to daughters, do not to sons"

(89) 能X不能Y neng2/can X bu4/not neng2/can Y

企业能活不能死
qi3ye4/enterprise neng2/can huo2/alive bu4/not neng2/can si3/die
"a bankrupt of this enterprise is not allowed"

(90) 宜X不宜Y yi2/should_be X bu4/not yi2/should_be

政制发展宜缓不宜急
zheng4/political zhi3/system fa1zheng3/development yi2/should_be huan3/slow bu2/not yi2/should_be ji2/hurry
"the development of political system should not be hurried but take some more time"

The gap between English frames and Chinese frames is sometimes caused as one meaning in English can be realized by several different Chinese words, such as "from X to Y" (Transitional Antonymy) being found in:

(91) 由X趋Y *you2/from X qu1/to Y*

由弱趋强 *you2/from ruo4/weak qu1/to qiang2/strong* "becoming stronger"

(92) 先X后Y *xian1/first X hou4/then Y*

先急后缓 *xian1/first ji2/fast hou4/then huan3/slow* "hurry at first then slow down"

(93) 由X到Y *you2/from X dao4/to Y*

由小到大 *you2/from xiao3/small dao4/to da4/big* "being biger"

The meaning of "from" is realized by *you2* or *xian1*, and the meaning of "to" is then translated to *qu1* or *hou3* or *dao4*.

And, sometimes it is because of the lexicalized meaning of words. For example, 讴歌X鞭笞Y *ou1ge2/eulogize X bian1chi4/flog Y* is listed as a frame of Negated Antonymy in Chinese, because, on one hand, *ou1ge1* literally means "(to) sing the praises" and here it is understood as "(to) eulogize", which contains the meaning of "(to) support"; on the other hand, the literal meaning of *bian1chi4* is "lash and knout" and here it is used as a verb for the meaning of "(to) fight fiercely against something". Such usages are common in Chinese but the English frames sometimes do not have their equals, proving the necessity to build a list of Chinese syntactic frames, based on the sample experiment we have.

Another example of the gap between the Chinese frame list and English one is "noun 愈/越 X noun 愈/越Y" ("noun is more X and noun is more Y"). The literal meaning of such frame is "(when) something/someone be more X, (then) something/someone be more Y". Since it is always required to have two contrasts in this frame, it is tagged as Ancillary Antonymy.

In the Chinese sample test, we also find that, for some pairings, it is common to have the pairing co-occurrence with numbers, such as, 两大一小 *liang3/two da4/big yi1/one xiao3/small*, 三男一女 *san1/three nan2/man yi1/one nv3/woman*. We tag them as a new category: Numeric Opposite.

In the sample test, we generalize over 200 independent frames. The frames like "X 和 (*he2*) Y", "X同 (*tong2/and*) Y""X以及 (*yi3ji2/and*) Y", "X还有 (*hai2you3/and*) Y" all mean "X and Y" and share the same syntactic structure, so they are combined as "X和|同|以及|......|还有 Y" as one frame. An example of the syntactic frames we have in the main experiment is listed here[2] (Table 4.5).

Basic Constraints in Experiment

In order to make sure of a high precision of extracted sentences, we add some constraints to the syntactic patterns.

a. **window size**

In order to control the accuracy of extracted data, we restrict the window size to one sentence. That is to say, only the collocation of candidate pairings within one sentence can be extracted out as an example. Any collocations beyond the window size; that is, being separated by a full stop mark, a question mark, exclamatory mark or suspension points, will be automatically excluded.

b. **trigger words**

In some of the frames, the trigger words are fixed, like:

"w=(什么) w=(是) w=({0}) punct{0,1} w=(什么) w=(是) w=({1})"

As we can see clearly, the trigger words in this pattern are 什么 (shen2 me0, *what or which*) and 是*shi4/BE.*

In some other frames, the trigger words could be a category of POS, for example:

"noun w=(是){0,1} w=({0}) punct{0,1} noun w=(是){0,1} w=({1})"

The first word of the extracted sentences should be a noun and there should be another noun between the candidate pairing word and 是*shi4/BE.*

Some frames offered a general category for the trigger words but also restrict which words they could not be. Frames of this kind usually are:

"(adj|adv) w=({0}) w=(,|;){0,1} (adj|adv) w=({1})"; word0!=不, word3!=不

---

[2]In the following parts of our writing, the taggers of X and Y were replaced by A and –A, and the term 'antonymy' Jones (2002) used was changed to 'opposite', in order to keep consistent with our experiment design.

Table 4.5 Syntactic frames used in Chinese experiment in discourse

<table>
<tr><th>Classes of opposite</th><th>Chinese syntactic frames[a]</th></tr>
<tr><td>Ancillary opposite</td><td>A 的有……, –A的有……;
noun A (,) noun –A;
A noun (,) –A noun;
……(是)A(的同时,)……(是) –A;
A了……, (却|但是|但|然而) –A 了……;
……越|更|愈A, ……越|更|愈 –A;</td></tr>
<tr><td>Coordinated opposite</td><td>A 和 –A;
A 到……, –A到……;
虽然A, 而又 –A;
verb A (,) verb –A;
可以(是)A, 也可以(是) –A;
不分 A –A;</td></tr>
<tr><td>Comparative opposite</td><td>A 多于|优于|不如|比|胜于|多于| –A;
A少于|低于|劣于|次于|不及 –A;</td></tr>
<tr><td>Distinguished opposite</td><td>什么是A, 什么是 –A;
有的A, 还有的 –A;
A 是……, –A是……;
时而 A, 时而–A;
A –A 之分;</td></tr>
<tr><td>Transitional opposite</td><td>从 A 到 –A
先 A 后 –A;
A 被 –A 所取代;</td></tr>
<tr><td>Negated opposite</td><td>宁愿A, (而|也|就)不愿意–A;
不但不(是)A, 反而(是) –A;
避A就–A;</td></tr>
<tr><td>Negated opposite</td><td>A不是|非 –A;
弘扬|颂扬|讴歌 A, 鞭挞|反对|抵制 –A;
verb A, 不verb –A (verb 1= verb2);</td></tr>
<tr><td>Extreme opposite</td><td>A则……, –A则……;
……则A, ……则 –A;
最A的是……, 最 –A的是……;</td></tr>
<tr><td>Numeric opposite</td><td>number A (,) number –A;</td></tr>
<tr><td>Others</td><td>……都A, 只有…… –A;
不 A 不 –A;
……</td></tr>
</table>

Appendix C offers a complete list of syntactic frames used in Chinese experiment, with examples

The two trigger words of this pattern were adj. or adv., but neither of them could be the word 不*bu4/no*.

Some frames do not have fixed trigger words but require the ones within the sentence should be the same:

"!punct w=({0}) w=(,|、|与|和|同|跟|以及|还有|连同|又) !punct w=({1})"; word0=word3, P0=any, P3=any

Here the first word and third word are used as trigger words. They are restricted to be identical within this frame.

c. **unknown words**

In order to extract the most useful examples, we have to set a maxim length to limit the number of the possible unknown words in the patterns. Generally, the length is set as 5 words. That is to say, there could be at most five unknown words between two known parts:

"w=({0}) w=(的) w=(有|是) !p=punct{1,5} punct{0,1} w=({1}) w=(的) w=(只有|只是|有|是)"

The part "!p=punct{1,5}" indicates that for this part of the frame, there could be one to five unknown words.

4.3 Result

In our experiment, 55 of 94 syntactic frames extract enough sentences (more than 10 sentences). 2662 pairings are extracted for examples. 21,207 sentences are extracted for 12 antonym groups; 57,065 sentences, for 5 complementary groups; and, 13,983 sentences, for 5 converse groups. We randomly select out 2,000 sentences from the extracted examples, and the precision of them is around 92% (Fig. 4.3).

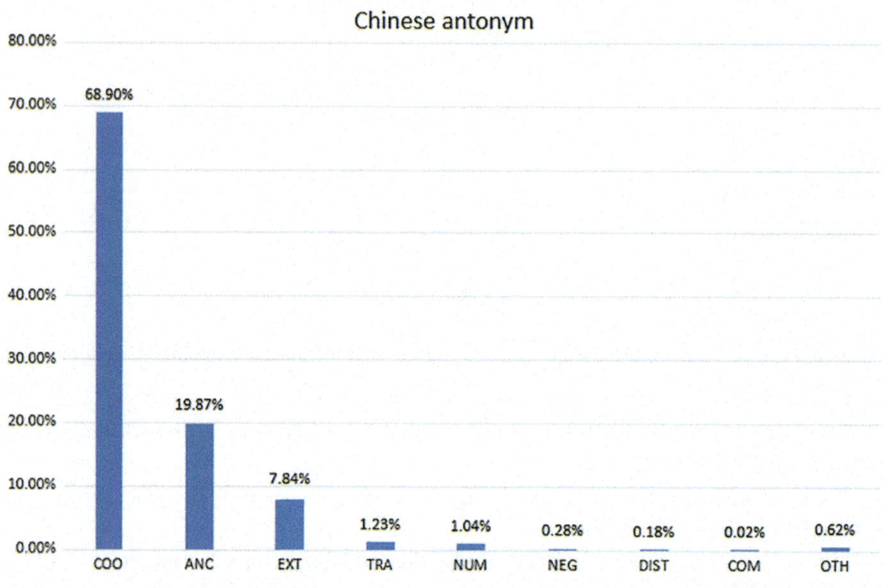

Fig. 4.3 Distribution of discourse functions in Chinese antonym category. Abbreviation: *COO* Coordinated opposite; *ANC* Ancillary opposite; *EXT* Extreme opposite; *TRA* Transitional opposite; *NUM* Numeric opposite; *NEG* Negated opposite; *DIST* Distinguished opposite; *COM* Comparative opposite; *OTH* others

4.3.1 Antonyms and Their Discourse Functions

In our Chinese corpus, for opposite pairings of antonym category, 68.92% of extracted sentences belong to the discourse function of Coordinated Opposite. It is much higher than the second function, Ancillary Opposite, with 19.87%. Extreme Opposite is the third common discourse function, having a percentage of 7.84%. It is followed by Transitional Opposite and Numeric Opposite, with 1.23% and 1.04%, respectively. Compared to them, Negated Opposite, Distinguished Opposite and Comparative Opposite are not so common in the data. Only 0.28–0.02% of sentences are found in these functions. And the rest of the sentences, which cannot be classified into any of the discourse functions above, make up 0.62%.

Coordinated Opposite:

(1) 实行小私有化和大私有化方案

shi2xing2/execute xiao1/small si1you3hua4/privatization fang1an4/project he2/and da4/big si1you3hua4/privatization fang1an4/project
"to execute two different kinds of projects in privatization process"

(2) 小至电池,大到照相机

xiao3/small zhi4/to dian4chi2/battery, da4/big dao4/to zhao4xiang4ji1/camera
"from battery to camera"

(3) 战酷暑,斗严寒

zhan4/fight ku4/extremely shu3/hot, duo4/withstand yan2/severely han2/cold
'to fight with extremely hot and severely cold'

(4) 不论穷国富国

bu2lun4/no_matter qiong2/poor guo2/country fu4/rich guo2/country
"no matter poor country or rich country"

Ancillary Opposite:

(1) 冰山愈冷情愈热

bing1shan2/iceberg yu4/more leng3/cold qing2/emotion yu4/more re4/hot
"the more cold the iceberg is, the more hot (our) hearts are"

(2) 搞经济心要热,脑要冷

gao3/do jing1ji4/economy xin1/heart yao4/must re4/hot, nao3/brain yao4/must leng3/cold
"It is necessary to have both high passion and calm thinking in economic development."

(3) 江总书记强调抓好大型,放开放活小型

jiang1/Jiang zong3shu1ji4/General_Secretary qiang2diao4/emphasize zhua1/gasp hao3/good da4xing2/large, fang4/unleash kai1/open fang4/unleash huo2/alive xiao3xing2/small
"The General Secretary Jiang emphasized that (government should) closely control the large enterprises and cast off restrictions on small businesses."

(4) 个子小能量大

ge4zi0/height xiao3/small neng2liang4/energy da4/big
"small body with great energy"

Extreme Opposite:

(1) 最高温度可以达到摄氏四十多度，最低也有十几度

zui4/most gao2/high wen1du4/temperature ke3yi3/can da2dao4/achieve she4shi/centidegree si4shi2/forty duo1/more du4/degree, zui4/most di1/low ye3/also you3/have shi2ji3/around_ten du4/degree
"The highest temperature can achieve more than forty centidegree and even the lowest temperature still beyond ten centidegree."

(2) 亚洲消费最昂贵的城市是日本东京，物价最便宜的是印度孟买

ya4zhou1/Asia xiao1fei4/consumption zui4/most ang2gui4/expensive de0/DE cheng2shi4/city shi4/BE ri4ben3/Japan dong1jing1/Tokyo, wu4jia4/price zui4/most pian2yi4/cheap de0/DE shi4/BE yin4du4/India meng4mai3/Bombay
"In Asia, the most expensive city for consumption is Tokyo, Japan, while the cheapest one is Bombay, India."

Transitional Opposite:

(1) 由弱趋强

you2/from ruo4/weak qu1/to qiang2/strong
"to become stronger and stronger"

(2) 先冷后热

xian1/firstly leng3/cold hou4/then re4/hot
"to be cold at first, then become hot"

(3) 林场由小到大

lin2/forest chang3/field you1/from xiao3/small dao4/to da4/big
"the forest develops from small scale to large scale"

Numeric Opposite:

两大一小
liang3/two da4/big yi1/one xiao3/small
"two big and one small"

Negated Opposite:

(1) 削减的速度应该快而不是慢

xiao1jian3/cut_off de0/DE su4du4/speed ying1gai1/should kuai4/fast er2/but bu2shi3/not man4/slow
"the speed of cutting off should be not be slowed down but faster"

(2) 政制发展宜缓不宜急

zheng4/political zhi4/system fa1zhang3/development yi4/should huan3/slow bu4/not yi4/should ji2/fast
"the development of political system should be taken step by step, but not in a hurry"

(3) 住在海岛的人心情是宽阔、不狭隘

zhu4/live zai4/at hai3/sea dao3/island de0/DE ren2/people xin1qing2/feeling shi3/BE kuan1kuo3/open, bu3/not xia1ai4/narrow
"the people who live in islands share a broad minded heart, rather than a narrow one"

(4) 求慢不求快

qiu2/require man4/slow bu4/not qiu2/require kuai4/fast
"the pursuit of leisure but not quickness"

(5) 讴歌光明,鞭挞黑暗

ou1ge2/eulogize guang1ming2/brightness, bian1chi4/flog hei1an4/darkness
"to eulogize the positive sides and flog the negative sides"

Distinguished Opposite:

(1) 什么是聪明, 什么是愚蠢

shen2me0/what shi4/BE cong1ming2/clever, shen2me0/what shi4/BE yu2chun3/foolish
"what is clever, what is foolish"

(2) 高低不一

gao1/high di1/low bu4/not yi1/same
"do not share the same height"

(3) 同样类型的企业, 有的搞的好,有的搞的差

tong1yang4/same lei4xing2/kind de0/DE qi3ye4/enterprise, you3de0/some gao3/make de0/DE hao3/good, you3de0/some gao3/make de0/DE cha4/bad
"As to the same kind of enterprises, some of them are well managed while some others are bad managed."

Comparative Opposite:

好多于差
hao3/good duo1/more yu2/than cha4/bad
"good ones are more than bad ones"

Others:

(1) 以慢对快

yi3/use man4/slow dui4/to kuai4/fast
"to fight against a quick with a slow"

(2) 以小见大

yi3/use xiao3/small jian4/see da4/big
"to presume the whole body from a tiny part"

(3) 不高不低

bu4/not gao1/high bu4/not di1/low
"not too high or too low; the height is just right"

4.3.2 Complementary and Its Discourse Functions

The most common discourse function in Chinese complementary is Coordinated Opposite, with 83.83%—far more than the rest functions. The second one is Numeric Opposite, with only 7.76%. It is followed by Ancillary Opposite, with a percentage of 6.37%, and Comparative Opposite, with 1.11%, and Extreme Opposite, with 0.76%. Distinguished Opposite and Transitional Opposite take around 0.06–0.05%, a little bit higher than that of Negated Opposite, 0.04%. The rests sentences together take 0.14% of all the examples (Fig. 4.4).

Coordinated Opposite:

(1) 不论是真或者是假

bu2lun4/no_matter shi4/BE zhen1/true huo4zhe3/or shi4/BE jia3/false
"no matter it is true or false"

(2) 人从生到死,从生存环境到人的最后归宿都由他解释

ren2/people cong2/from sheng1/alive dao4/to si3/dead, cong2/from sheng1cun2/alive huan1jing4/environment dao4/to ren2/people de0/DE zui4hou4/last gui1su4/end dou1/all you2/by ta1/he jie3shi4/explain
"From existence to death, from living environment to the end-result of people, all of the things are explained by him."

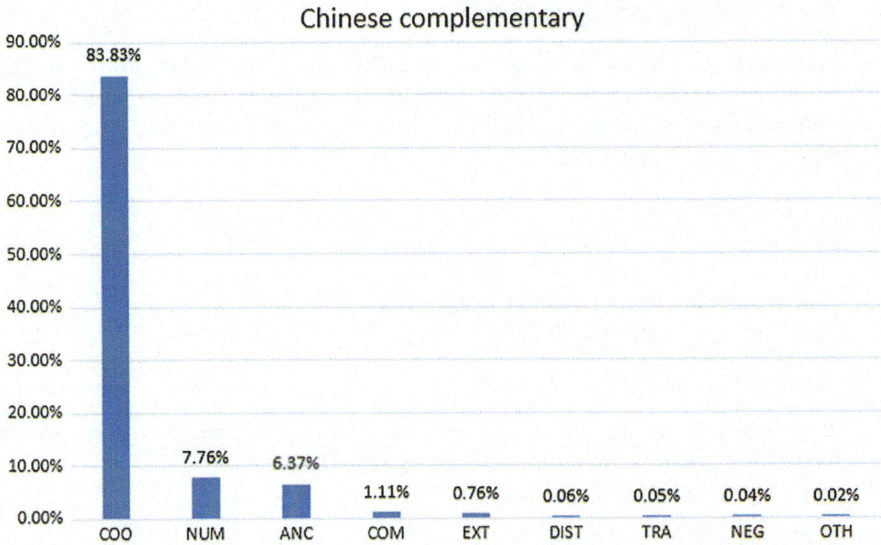

Fig. 4.4 Distribution of discourse functions in Chinese complementary category. Abbreviation: *COO* Coordinated opposite; *NUM* Numeric opposite; *ANC* Ancillary opposite; *COM* Comparative opposite; *EXT* Extreme Opposite; *DIST* Distinguished opposite; *TRA* Transitional opposite; *NEG* Negated opposite; *OTH* others

Numeric Opposite:

(1) 一真一假

yi1/one zhen1/true yi1/one jia3/false
"one true one false"

(2) 生还九十人,死亡十七人

sheng1/alive huan2/return jiu3shi2/ninety ren2/people, si3wang2/dead shi2qi1/seventeen ren2/people
"ninety people returned alive (but) seventeen ones dead"

Ancillary Opposite:

(1) 假集体真个体

jia3/false ji2ti3/collective zhen1/true ge4ti3/individual
"(to do something) for collective in name only (but) for individual in reality"

(2) 真汇票假数字

zhen1/true hui4piao4/bill jia3/false shu4zi4/number
"a valid bill with a fake number"

(3) 我们绝不能拆了真古迹,搞假古董

wo3men0/we ju2/must bu4/not neng2/should cha1/pull_down le0/LE zhen1/true gu3ji4/historical_sites, gao3/make jia3/false gu3dong3/antique
"We must not pull down the real historical sites at one hand while produce fake antiques at the other hand."

Comparative Opposite:

(1) 男少于女

nan2/male shao3/less yu2/than nv3/female
"there are less men than women"

(2) 当年那种生不如死的生活

dang1nian2/in_those_years na4/that zhong3/kind sheng1/alive bu4ru2/less_than si3/dead de0/DE sheng1huo2/life
"the miserable life in those years"

(3) 活着绝对比死了更有价值

huo2/alive zhe0/ZHE ju2dui4/definitely bi3/compare si3/dead le0/LE geng4/more you3/have jia4zhi2/value
"living is definitely more valuable than being dead"

Extreme Opposite:

(1) 合则强,分则弱

he2/together ze2/then qiang2/strong, fen1/separate ze2/then ruo4/weak
"staying together makes a strong unit while staying separately makes weak individuals"

(2) 爱得要死要活

ai4/love de0/DE yao4/want si3/death yao4/want huo2/living
"to experience suffering love"

(3) 法律是死的,人是活的

fa3lv4/law shi4/BE si3/dead de0/DE, ren2/people shi4/BE huo3/alive de0/DE
"the law is fixed while the operator of law is not"

Distinguished Opposite:

(1) 保安有"真""假"之分

bao3an1/security_guard you3/have zhen1/true jia3/false zhi1/DE fen1/distinguish
"there are real security guards and fake ones"

(2) 观察他究竟是生是死

guan1cha2/examine ta1/he jiu1jing4/indeed shi4/BE sheng1/alive shi4/BE si3/dead
"to examine that he is actually alive or dead"

(3) 他们有的已经过世,有的仍然健在

ta1men0/they you3de0/some yi3jing1/already guo4shi4/dead, you3de0/some reng2ran2/still jian4zai4/alive
"some of them already pass away while some others are still alive"

Transitional Opposite:

(1) 使得云溪化工厂起死回生

shi3de0/make yun2xi1/Yunxi hua4/chemistry gong1chang3/factory qi3/up si3/dead huo2/return sheng1/alive
"to bring Yunxi chemical factory back to life"

(2) 使4000多万元死钱变成了活钱

shi3/make 4000/4000 duo1/more wan4/ten_thousand si3/dead qian2/money bian4cheng2/change le0/LE huo2/alive qian2/money
"to make more than forty million fixed money become usable"

(3) 黑棋被吃的10子也死而复活

hei1/black qi2/chess_piece bei4/BEI chi1/eat de0/DE 10/10 zi3/piece ye3/too si3/dead er1/but fu4/again huo2/alive
"and, the ten surrounded stones of black group (in Go game) have the option to connect with friendly stones again"

(4) 变死知识为活知识

bian4/change si3/dead zhi1shi2/knowledge wei2/BE huo2/alive zhi1shi2/knowledge
"to apply theoretical knowledge into practical usage"

Negated Opposite

(1) 企业有生无死

qi3ye4/enterprise you3/have sheng1/alive wu2/no si3/dead
"once opened, any enterprise cannot be shut down"

(2) 传男不传女

chuan2/pass nan2/male bu4/not chuan2/pass nv3/female
"(it is) inherited by male children only"

(3) 工厂能开不能关等严重问题

gong1chang3/factory neng2/can kai1/open bu4/not neng2/can guan1/closed deng3/and_so_on yan2zhong4/serious wen4ti2/problem
"some severe problems such as once a factory is built then it can never be shut down"

Others:

(1) 半死不活

ban4/half si3/dead bu4/not huo2/alive
"half dead half alive"

(2) 半真半假

ban4/half zhen1/true ban4/half jia3/false
"half true and half false"

(3) 死去活来

si3/dead qu4/go huo2/alive lai2/come
"half dead half alive"

4.3.3 Converses and Their Discourse Functions

For Chinese converse, the most common discourse function is Coordinated Opposite, which takes 73.46%. Extreme Opposite takes 18.48% of all examples, in this opposite category. Ancillary Opposite is in the third position, with 6.86%. Comparative Opposite takes 0.05%. Transitional Opposite, Negated Opposite, Distinguished Opposite, Numeric Opposite and others together take 0.08% of all sentences. However, the examples which cannot be categorized into the eight discourse functions take about 1.06%, higher than that of Comparative Opposite, Transitional Opposite, Negated Opposite, Distinguished Opposite or Numeric Opposite and others (Fig. 4.5).
Coordinated Opposite:

(1) 不光是卖不难,买也不难

bu4guang1/not_only shi4/BE mai4/sell bu4/not nan2/difficulty, mai3/buy ye3/too bu4/not nan2/difficulty
"not only easy to sell but also easy to buy"

(2) 收购和销售血浆的行为

shou1gou4/buy he2/and xiao1shou4/sell xue3jiang1/plasma de0/DE xing2wei2/action
"the trade of plasma"

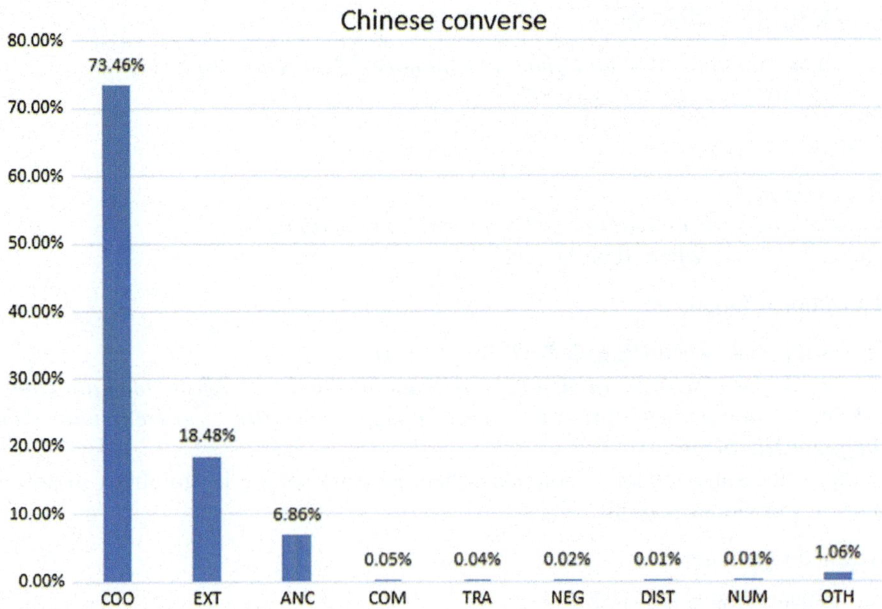

Fig. 4.5 Distribution of discourse functions in Chinese converse category. Abbreviation: *COO* Coordinated opposite; *EXT* Extreme opposite; *ANC* Ancillary opposite; *COM* Comparative opposite; *TRA* Transitional opposite; *NEG* Negated opposite; *DIST* Distinguished opposite; *NUM* Numeric opposite; *OTH* others

(3) 通过深入学习和教育

tong1guo4/via shen1ru4/deep xue2xi2/learn he2/and jiao4yu4/teaching
"via in depth education"

Extreme Opposite:

高价买进低价卖出
gao1/high jia4/price mai3/buy jin4/in di1/low jia4/price mai4/sell chu1/out
"buying at a high price (but) selling out at a low price"

Ancillary Opposite:

(1) 国际对冲基金继续抛售美元, 购进日元

guo2ji4/international dui4chong1/hedge ji1jin1/fund ji4xu4/continue pao1shou4/sell mei3yuan2/U.S._dollar, gou4jin4/buy ri4yuan2/Japanese_yen
"international hedge funds continue selling U.S. dollars and buying yen"

(2) 收买时间、出卖空间

shou1mai3/buy shi2jian1/time, chu1mai4/sell kong1jian1/space
"to buy time and sell spaces"

Comparative Opposite:

卖的多过买的
mai4/sell de0/DE duo1/more yu2/than mai3/buy de0/DE
"there are more sellers than buyers"

Transitional Opposite:

使公司经营从目前的店面零售改为个人订购
shi3/make gong1si1/enterprise jing1ying2/management cong2/from mu4qian2/now de0/DE dian4mian4/storefront gai3/change wei2/BE ge4ren2/individual ding4gou4/booking
"to have the sales model of company changed from selling in storefront in nowadays to individual booking"

Negated Opposite:

(1) 营销的本质是买, 不是卖

ying2xiao1/sell de0/DE ben3zhi4/essence shi4/BE mai3/buy, bu4/not shi4/BE mai4/sell
"the essence of trade is what to buy but not how to sell"

(2) 改变目前黄金只能买进不能卖出的现象

gai3bian4/change mu4qian2/now huang2jin1/gold zhi3neng2/only mai3jin4/buy bu4/not neng2/can mai4chu1/sell de0/DE xian4xiang4/situation
"to change the situation that in nowadays gold can only be bought in but not sold out"

(3) 也有人认为其股价已被高估而只能抛不能买

ye3/and you3/have ren2/people ren4wei2/think qi2/its gu3/stock jia4/price yi3/already bei4/BEI gao1gu1/over_valued er2/then zhi3neng2/only pao1/sell bu4/not neng1/can mai3/buy
"there are also some people think that its stock price has been over valued that it can only be sold rather than bought"

Distinguished Opposite:

交易会以订货为主、销售为辅
jiao1yi4/trade hui4/meeting yi3/use ding4 huo4/buy wei2/BE zhu3/major, xiao1shou4/sell wei2/BE fu3/minor
"the trade fair is mainly for booking goods, rather than selling things directly"

Numeric Opposite:

(1) SPC 购买受创国发行的一百亿美元公债每年可获得利息收入十亿美元

SPC/SPC gou4mai3/buy shou4chuang4/injured guo2/country fa1xing2/issue de0/DE yi1bai3/one_hundred yi4/one_hundred_million mei3yuan2/U.S._dollar gong1zhai4/public_loan mai3/every nian2/year ke3/can huo4de2/earn li4xi1/interests shou1ru4/income shi2/ten yi4/one_hundred_million mei3yuan2/U.S._dollar

"the ten billion U.S. dollars' public loans of injured country bring SPC one billion dollars' interests every year"

(2) 近几年来先后卖掉了50多头大畜,购进了200多只纯白山羊

jin4/near ji3/several nian2/year lai2/come xian1hou4/early_or_late mai4diao4/sell le0/LE 50/50 duo1/more tou2/CL da4/big chu4/animal, gou4jin4/buy le0/LE 200/200 duo1/more zhi1/CL chun2/pure bai2/white shan1yang2/goat

"in recent years, (they) sold more than fifty big animals to buy around two hundred pure white goats"

Others:

(1) 不来不去

bu4/not lai2/come bu4/not qu4/go

"staying unmoved"

(2) 拍卖在激烈的竞买中进行

pai1mai4/auction zai4/at ji1lie4/competitive de0/DE jing4mai4/fight_for_buying zhong1/in_the_process jin4xing2/go_on

"the auction is competitive"

(3) 教学相长

jiao4/teach xue2/study xiang1/together zhang3/grow

"teachers and students help each other to become better"

4.4 Discussion

4.4.1 Comparison of Antonym, Complementary and Converse

As we can see from this figure, the distributions of the three opposite sub-types in discourse functions are close in many points. First of all, the Coordinated Opposite is the most frequent discourse function across all the three sub-types of Chinese

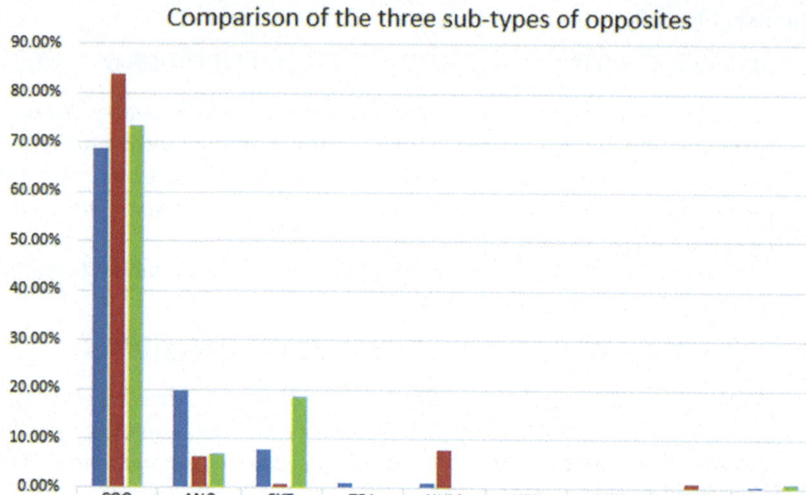

	COO	ANC	EXT	TRA	NUM	NEG	DIST	COM	OTH
antonym	68.90%	19.87%	7.84%	1.23%	1.04%	0.28%	0.18%	0.02%	0.62%
complementary	83.83%	6.37%	0.76%	0.05%	7.76%	0.04%	0.06%	1.11%	0.02%
converse	73.46%	6.86%	18.48%	0.04%	0.01%	0.02%	0.01%	0.05%	1.06%

antonym complementary converse

Fig. 4.6 Comparison of discourse function distributions in Chinese antonym, complementary and converse categories. Abbreviation: *COO* Coordinated opposite; *ANC* Ancillary opposite; *EXT* Extreme opposite; *TRA* Transitional opposite; *NUM* Numeric opposite; *NEG* Negated opposite; *DIST* Distinguished opposite; *COM* Comparative opposite; *OTH* others

opposite, taking at least 70% of the antonym, complementary and converse categories. In the fourth position, Transitional Opposites occupies a similar percentage in all the three types. Additionally, Negated Opposite, Distinguished Opposite, Comparative Opposite and others take a close percentage in the sixth, seventh, eighth and ninth positions, respectively. The three categories vary in the rank of second most frequent discourse function. For antonym, it was Ancillary Opposite, at around 20%; for complementary, Numeric Opposite, at a little bit less than 10%; for converse, Extreme Opposite, also at around 20%. As to the third most frequent function, for antonym, it is Extreme Opposite; for complementary and converse, Ancillary Opposite (Fig. 4.6).

This figure shows that the basic distributions of the three sub-types are not the same. Coordinated Opposite is the most common function across all three types, and has a much more overwhelming percentage than the other eight functions in complementary. Compared with antonym and complementary, converse has a higher percentage in Extreme Opposite. And, Numeric Opposite is much more common in complementary than in antonym or converse. The function distributions of antonym and converse are more similar to each other than that of complementary.

4.4.2 Comparison of Chinese, English and Japanese Antonym

Then, we compare the results of Chinese antonyms with that of English (Jones 2002) and of Japanese (Muehleisen and Isono 2009) (Fig. 4.7).

According to the results, the discourse functions are applicable to Chinese data. The functions defined by Jones (2002) take the majority of the data and only 1.86% of sentences left as other categories. And, as the above figure and table show, Coordinated Opposite and Ancillary Opposite are the most common functions in all three languages. In English, their percentages are almost the same. However in Chinese, Coordinated Opposite is much higher than Ancillary Opposite; while in Japanese, the situation is reverse. Extreme Opposite in Chinese has 7.84%, but only around 1% in English and Japanese. Transitional Opposite has 8.67% in Japanese but only 3% in English and 1.23% in Chinese. Around 2% of examples in both English and Japanese are classified into Negated Opposite, however, in our Chinese experiment, only 0.28% of extracted sentences belong to the same category. Over 98% of Chinese examples could be explained by the five main function categories while around 20% of examples in English and Japanese are categorized as the rest categories.

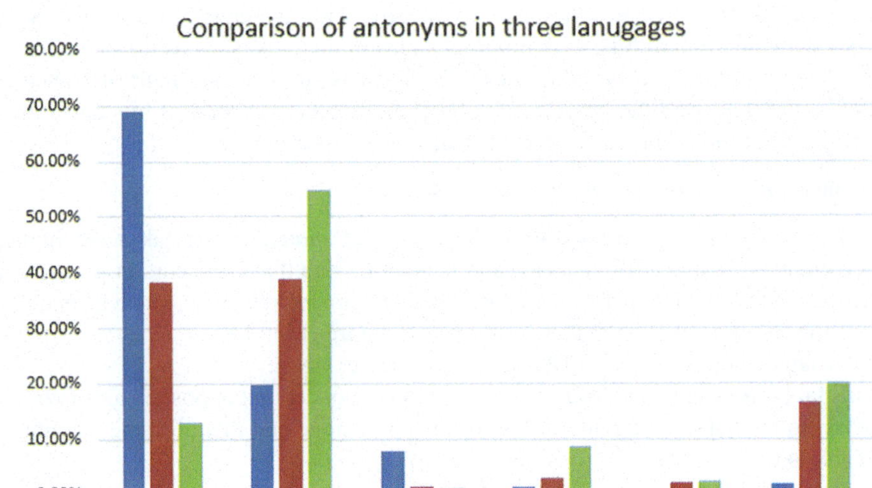

	COO	ANC	EXT	TRA	NEG	the rests
Chinese	68.92%	19.87%	7.84%	1.23%	0.28%	1.86%
English	38.37%	38.73%	1.33%	3.00%	2.07%	16.50%
Japanese	13.00%	54.83%	1.00%	8.67%	2.33%	20.17%

Fig. 4.7 Comparison of discourse function distributions of Chinese, English and Japanese antonym

4.4.3 *Canonical Opposite*

Our Measurement on Canonicity

$$\text{Dominance-Score(D-Score)} = \sqrt{(\text{percentage of hits} * \text{percentage of frames} * 100)}$$
$$= \sqrt{\left(\frac{\text{hits of pairing}}{\text{all hits of group}} * \frac{\text{frames of pairing}}{\text{all frame of group}} * 100\right)}$$

The Dominance-Score (D-Score) is used to measure the canonicity of one opposite pairing. It is decided by two factors: the hit number and the distribution of syntactic frames. If the D-Score were 5 or more, the matched pairing is defined as a canonical one.

4.4.3.1 Two Case Studies

Basically, within the same conceptual pair, the percentage of a frame goes down with the reduction of hits. In other words, the more frequently one pairing members co-occur, the more frames they tend to occupy. And, the general trend of D-Score goes with the trend of hits, with minor changes in the rank, such as the one which is third most frequent in hits then takes the forth position in the rank of D-Scores. Following this, we offer two case studies: one for the harmony of hits and frames percentages; the other, for the conflict of the two percentages.

A harmonious case: ***strong versus weak***

From the figure, we can see that, the paring of *qiang2: ruo4* takes the highest percentage of extracted sentences, and is also the one that co-occurs in most of the frames. When the hits percentage decreases, the frames percentage also goes down, and the two lines keep parallel in the whole figure (Fig. 4.8).
Next table shows the rank of D-Score for *strong: weak.*
This table shows the rank of D-Score, within the conceptual opposite pair of *strong: weak*, follows the same rank of that of hits percentage and that of frame percentage (Table 4.6).

A conflictive case: ***receive versus give***

In the figure for *receive: give*, however, we can see that the trends of hits percentage and frames percentage are not parallel to each other. *Zheng1qv3: fang4qi4* is the pairing co-occurring in the largest percentage of extracted sentences, but it is not the one which has the widest distribution in frames. The one with widest distribution of frames is *qv3: she3*, in the third position of hit rank. *Huang4qv3: fang3qi4* is the

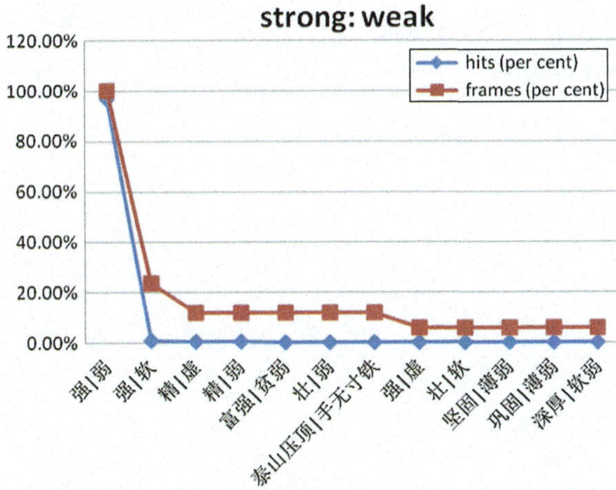

Fig. 4.8 Comparison between percentages of individual token and pattern in *Strong: Weak*

Table 4.6 Dominance score of individual pairings in case of *Strong: Weak*

Rank	Pairing	D-Score	Hits	Frames
1	强|弱	9.84	959 (96.77%)	17 (100.00%)
2	强|软	0.51	11 (1.11%)	4 (23.53%)
3	精|虚	0.24	5 (0.50%)	2 (11.76%)
4	精|弱	0.22	4 (0.40%)	2 (11.76%)
5	富强|贫弱	0.19	3 (0.30%)	2 (11.76%)
6	壮|弱	0.15	2 (0.20%)	2 (11.76%)
7	泰山压顶|手无寸铁	0.15	2 (0.20%)	2 (11.76%)
8	强|虚	0.08	1 (0.10%)	1 (5.88%)
9	壮|软	0.08	1 (0.10%)	1 (5.88%)
10	坚固|薄弱	0.08	1 (0.10%)	1 (5.88%)
11	巩固|薄弱	0.08	1 (0.10%)	1 (5.88%)
12	深厚|软弱	0.08	1 (0.10%)	1 (5.88%)
		Total	991	17

most frequent pairing in sentences, but fourth in frames distribution. Hence, in the table X, *qv3: she3* replaces *huang4qv3: fang4qi4* in the second position of the D-Score rank. We also notice that the sixth most frequently co-occurring pairing, *huo4de2: qi4quan2*, taking significantly less frames than its followers, *duo2qv3: fang4qi4*, *na2dao4: diu1qi4* and so on. So it is unsurprising to see its D-Score rank dropping to tenth (Fig. 4.9 and Table 4.7).

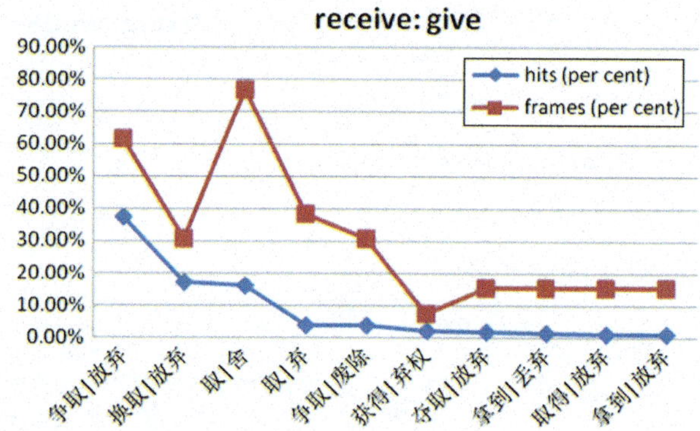

Fig. 4.9 Comparison between percentages of individual token and pattern in *Receive: Give*

Table 4.7 Dominance score of individual pairings in *Receive: Give*

Rank	Pairing	D-Score	Hits (%)	Frames (%)
1	争取|放弃	4.80	290 (37.32%)	8 (61.54%)
2	取|舍	3.52	125 (16.09%)	10 (76.92%)
3	换取|放弃	2.29	133 (17.12%)	4 (30.77%)
4	取|弃	1.24	31 (3.99%)	5 (38.46%)
5	争取|废除	1.07	29 (3.73%)	4 (30.77%)
6	夺取|放弃	0.53	14 (1.80%)	2 (15.38%)
7	拿到|丢弃	0.47	11 (1.42%)	2 (15.38%)
8	取得|放弃	0.44	10 (1.29%)	2 (15.38%)
9	拿到|放弃	0.42	9 (1.16%)	2 (15.38%)
…	…	…	…	…
60	拿到|废弃	0.10	1(0.129%)	1(7.69%)
		Total	777	13

4.4.3.2 Top 5 Pairings of All Candidate Pairs

Group A

In the 22 opposite concepts, 16 out of them have one canonical pairing. They are (Table 4.8):

Huo2: si3 ("alive: dead"), *nan2: nv3* ("male: female"), *zhen1: jia3* ("true: false"), *kai1: guan1* ("open: close"), *ji1: ou3* ("odd: even"), *kuai4: man4* ("fast: slow"), *qiang2: ruo4* ("strong: weak"), *da4: xiao3* ("big: small"), *kuan1: zhai3* ("wide: narrow"), *hao3: huai4* ("good: bad"), *hou4: bo2* ("thick: thin"), *da4: di1* ("expensive: cheap"), *pang4: shou4* ("fat: slim"), *mei3: chou3* ("beautiful: ugly"), *lai2: qu4* ("come: go"), *juan1zeng4: jia1shou4* ("give: receive").

We also notice that, within these 16 pairs, some of the so-called canonical pairings, however, are not accepted in certain contexts. For example, for the opposite group of "fat: slim", the pairs of *pang4: shou4* and *cu1: xi4* are close in

Table 4.8 Top 5 canonical pairings in 22 conceptual opposite groups

		D-Score rank 1	2	3	4	5
Complementary	生: 死	活: 死 (7.07);	生: 死 (2.72);	生存: 死亡 (1.12);	生还: 死亡 (0.84);	生还: 丧生 (0.51)
	男: 女	男: 女 (5.31);	男子: 女子 (2.96);	男性: 女性 (2.31);	子: 女 (1.01);	男人: 女人 (0.95)
	真: 假	真: 假 (7.28);	实: 虚 (3.27);	真实: 虚假(1.19);	真: 幻 (0.69);	真实: 虚伪(0.42)
	开: 合	开: 关 (6.67);	打开: 关闭(2.37);	开: 闭 (1.84);	开启: 关闭(1.51);	展: 关 (0.80)
	奇: 偶	双: 单 (9.60);	双数: 单数(1.22);	偶数: 奇数(0.53);	双: 独 (0.43);	偶: 独 (0.31)
Antonym	快: 慢	快: 慢 (6.31);	急: 缓 (2.59);	急性: 慢性(2.01);	速: 慢 (1.13);	急: 慢 (0.86)
	明: 暗	光明: 黑暗 (4.95);	明: 暗 (4.50);	亮: 暗 (2.01);	亮: 黑 (1.78);	明: 黑 (1.03)
	强: 弱	强: 弱 (9.84);	强: 软 (0.51);	精: 虚 (0.24);	精: 弱 (0.22);	富强: 贫弱(0.19)
	大: 小	大: 小 (9.78);	大型: 小型(0.91);	大: 细 (0.34);	大: 纤 (0.19);	大型: 微型(0.14)
	宽: 窄	宽: 窄 (7.79);	广: 窄 (0.79);	宽敞: 狭小 (0.79);	宽广: 狭窄(0.68);	宽大: 狭隘(0.68)
	好: 坏	好: 坏 (5.27);	好: 差 (2.93);	优: 劣 (2.05);	佳: 差 (0.73);	好: 糟 (0.63)
	厚: 薄	厚: 薄 (7.78);	浓: 淡 (2.68);	浓: 稀 (1.81);	腻: 淡 (0.57);	稠: 稀 (0.47)
	冷: 热	寒冷: 酷热 (3.97);	寒冷: 炎热(2.56);	严寒: 酷热(2.15);	冰冷: 火热(1.62);	冰冷: 炎热(1.15)
	贵: 贱	大: 低 (9.05);	贵: 贱 (0.88);	高昂: 低下(0.59);	惠: 低 (0.53);	昂贵: 便宜(0.32)
	肥: 瘦	胖: 瘦 (6.29);	粗: 细 (5.05);	丰满: 苗条(0.93);	肥胖: 苗条(0.57);	肥胖: 纤细(0.44)
	美: 丑	美: 丑 (6.12);	美丽: 丑陋(4.68);	漂亮: 丑陋(2.65);	好看: 难看(1.25);	华丽: 难看(1.25)
	智: 愚	明白: 糊涂 (4.08);	聪明: 愚拙(1.77);	敏锐: 笨拙(1.77);	聪明: 愚蠢(1.67);	敏感: 迟钝(1.44)
Converse	买: 卖	买进: 卖出 (3.02);	购买: 出售(1.63);	购: 销 (1.44);	买入: 卖出(1.39);	采购: 销售(1.22)
	来: 去	来: 去 (8.35);	过来: 过去(0.60);	前来: 前往(0.57);	光顾: 前往(0.54);	来到: 前往(0.41)
	教: 学	教育: 学习 (4.97);	辅导: 学习(1.98);	指导: 学习(1.93);	辅导: 就学(1.65);	教导: 学习(1.62)
	取: 舍	争取: 放弃 (4.80);	取: 舍 (3.52);	换取: 放弃(2.29);	取: 弃 (1.24);	争取: 废除(1.07)
	施: 受	捐赠: 接受 (7.22);	赠送: 接受(2.76);	赠与: 接受(2.01);	给: 受 (1.45);	捐赠: 收受(1.45)

D-Score, but *pang4: shoud4* usually used to describe the body shape of humans, such as:

(94) 两位嫌犯一胖、一瘦

liang3/two wei4/CL xian2fan4/suspect yi1/one pang4/fat, yi1/one shou4/slim
"one of the two suspects is fat while the other one is slim"
* 两位嫌犯一粗、一细
liang3/two wei4/CL xian2fan4/suspect yi1/one cu2/thick, yi1/one xian4/thin
"one of the two suspects is fat while the other one is slim"

And, for shape of food, plants and things other than humans, it is more acceptable to use *cu1: xi4*:

(95) 厨师可以做出粗细不等的拉面

chu2shi1/cook ke2yi3 zuo4/make chu1/out cu1/thick xi4/thin bu4/not deng3/equal de0/DE la1mian4/hand-pulled_noodles
"The cook can make thick or thin Hand-pulled Noodles"
* 厨师可以做出胖瘦不等的拉面
chu2shi1/cook ke2yi3 zuo4/make chu1/out pang4/fat shou4/slim bu4/not deng3/equal de0/DE la1mian4/hand-pulled_noodles
"The cook can make thick or thin Hand-pulled Noodles"

(96) 长有一粗一细两个树身

zhang3/grow you3/have yi1/one cu2/thick yi1/one xian4/thin liang3/two ge4/CL shu4/tree shen1/body
"(it) has two boles, one is thick and one is thin"
* 长有一胖一瘦两个树身[3]
zhang3/grow you3/have yi1/one pang4/fat yi1/one shou4/slim liang3/two ge4/CL shu4/tree shen1/body
"(it) has two boles, one is thick and one is thin"

In the conceptual opposite group of male: female, the collocation of *nan2: nv3, nan2zi3: nv3zi3* and *nan2xing4: nv3xing4* occupy different frames:

(97) 韩国是男尊女卑的社会

han2guo2/Korea shi4/BE nan2/male zun1/respectable nv3/female bei1/insignificant
"Man is superior to woman in Korea"
* 韩国是男子尊女子卑的社会
han2guo2/Korea shi4/BE nan2zi3/male zun1/respectable nv3zi3/female bei1/insignificant
"Man is superior to woman in Korea"
? 韩国是男性尊女性卑的社会

[3]This saying is acceptable only if it's a metaphor of human.

han2guo2/Korea shi4/BE nan2xing4/male zun1/respectable nv3xing4/female bei1/insignificant
"Man is superior to woman in Korea"

(98) 新疆杂技团的五男二女共七名演员

xin1jiang1/Xinjiang za2ji4tuan2/acrobatics_troupe de0/DE wu3/five nan2/male er4/two nv3/female tong4/together qi1/seven ming2/CL yan3yuan2/trouper
"There are five male and two female troupers in Xinjiang Acrobatics Troupe"
* 新疆杂技团的五男子二女子共七名演员
xin1jiang1/Xinjiang za2ji4tuan2/acrobatics_troupe de0/DE wu3/five nan2zi3/male er4/two nv3zi3/female tong4/together qi1/seven ming2/CL yan3yuan2/trouper
"There are five male and two female troupers in Xinjiang Acrobatics Troupe"
? 新疆杂技团的五男性二女性共七名演员
xin1jiang1/Xinjiang za2ji4tuan2/acrobatics_troupe de0/DE wu3/five nan2xing4/male er4/two nv3xing4/female tong4/together qi1/seven ming2/CL yan3yuan2/trouper
"There are five male and two female troupers in Xinjiang Acrobatics Troupe"

(99) 男子双杠及女子高低杠

nan2zi3/male shuang1gang4/parallel_bars ji2/and nv3zi3/femaleshuang1 gang4/parallel_bars
"Men's Parallel Bars and Women's Parallel Bars"
* 男双杠及女高低杠
nan2/male shuang1gang4/parallel_bars ji2/and nv3/female shuang1gang4/parallel_bars
"Men's Parallel Bars and Women's Parallel Bars"
* 男性双杠及女性高低杠
nan2xing4/male shuang1gang4/parallel_bars ji2/and nv3xing4/female shuang1gang4/parallel_bars
"Men's Parallel Bars and Women's Parallel Bars"

(100) 男女配对组只有男子六人和女子三人报名参加

nan2/male nv3/female pei4dui4/matched zu4/group zhi3/only you3/have nan2zi3/male
liu4/six ren2/CL he2/and nv3zi3/female san1/three ren2/CL bao4ming2/apply can1jia1/participate
"There are only six men and three women applying for the mixed group"
? 男女配对组只有男六人和女三人报名参加

nan2/male nv3/female pei4dui4/matched zu4/group zhi3/only you3/have nan2/male liu4/six ren2/CL he2/and nv3/female san1/three ren2/CL bao4ming2/apply can1jia1/participate
"There are only six men and three women applying for the mixed group"
? 男女配对组只有男性六人和女性三人报名参加
nan2/male nv3/female pei4dui4/matched zu4/group zhi3/only you3/have nan2xing4/male liu4/six ren2/CL he2/and nv3xing4/female san1/three ren2/CL bao4ming2/apply can1jia1/participate
"There are only six men and three women applying for the mixed group"

(101) 男性较女性适合当总统

nan2xing4/male jiao4/compare nv3xing4/female shi4he2/suitable dang1/BE zong3tong3/president
"Male is more suitable than woman to be president."
* 男较女适合当总统

nan2/male jiao4/compare nv3/female shi4he2/suitable dang1/BE zong3 tong3/president
"Male is more suitable than woman to be president."

? 男子较女子适合当总统

nan2zi3/male jiao4/compare nv3zi3/female shi4he2/suitable dang1/BE zong3tong3/president
"Male is more suitable than woman to be president."

(102) 欧洲人平均寿命为男性六十七点五岁、女性七十三点四岁

ou1zhou1/Europe ren2/people ping2jun1/average shou4ming4/life_ expectancy wei2/BE nan2xing4/male liu4shi2qi1dian3wu3/67.5 sui4/year, nv3xing4/female qi1shi2san1dian3si4/73.4 sui4/year
"The average life expectancy of European is 67.5 years for male and 73.4 years for female."
? 欧洲人平均寿命为男六十七点五岁、女七十三点四岁
ou1zhou1/Europe ren2/people ping2jun1/average shou4ming4/life_ expectancy wei2/BE nan2/male liu4shi2qi1dian3wu3/67.5 sui4/year, nv3/female qi1shi2san1dian3si4/73.4 sui4/year
"The average life expectancy of European is 67.5 years for male and 73.4 years for female."
? 欧洲人平均寿命为男子六十七点五岁、女子七十三点四岁
ou1zhou1/Europe ren2/people ping2jun1/average shou4ming4/life_ expectancy wei2/BE nan2zi3/male liu4shi2qi1dian3wu3/67.5 sui4/year, nv3zi3/female qi1shi2san1dian3si4/73.4 sui4/year
"The average life expectancy of European is 67.5 years for male and 73.4 years for female."

It suggests that, being a canonical pairing does not mean it can replace the other pairings in all the contexts. Canonical pairings are only relatively more frequent in co-occurrence and syntactic frame distribution in general but in certain contexts a particular pairing, rather than the canonical one, would be chosen.

Group B

For the rest 6 opposite concept pairs, the D-Scores of the top 5 pairings closely followed each other. Hence it is hard to define which one is dominating in both hit number and syntactic frame distribution. In other words, none of the candidate pairings had a significantly higher frequency (around or more than 50%) or wider syntactic frame distribution (around or more than 50%). We might say that the candidate pairings, within such conceptual groups, are still in the competition to be canonical. The 6 groups are: "bright: dark", "cold: hot", "clever: foolish", "buy: sell", "teach: learn" and "accept: offer".

The later three of them are all converse pairs. Since there are only 5 converse pairs in our study and 3 of them are without a canonical pairing, it is safe to say that converse pairs, compared with that of complementary and antonym, are more unlikely to have canonical pairings.

The findings of our experiment suggest that it is possible for a conceptual opposite group to have canonical pairing. Sometimes, the canonical pairing takes a significant advantage in both frequency and syntactic frame distribution, and therefore dominantly leads the other possible pairings. In some other cases, the leading advantage is not so obvious, although it is easy to select which pairing is canonical. Sometimes, there are several pairings that take relatively equal positions in canonicity. Since in such cases, the preferred domain(s) of these pairings usually differ from each, they might be termed as canonical pairings in independent domains. And, in some opposite groups, extracted sentences are so dispersed in different candidate pairings that none of the pairings can be called canonical.

Hence, the general mark of "there is a scale of canonicity from 'good ones' to 'bad ones'", by previous experimental studies (Jones 2007; Paradis et al. 2006, 2009; Williners and Paradis 2010; Jones et al. 2012), does not perfectly go with our experiment data. Meanwhile, our result may follow the earlier dated view (Herrmann et al. 1979) of canonicity being non-dichotomous. The data from Chinese experiment is somewhere in between the two views. Canonical pairings do not appear in every conceptual opposite group; and, the curve of canonicity vary in different groups, it is not in a continuum but has a sudden drop with the canonical pairing and the rest. And, converse pairs are more unlikely to have canonical pairings than the other two sub-types of opposites.

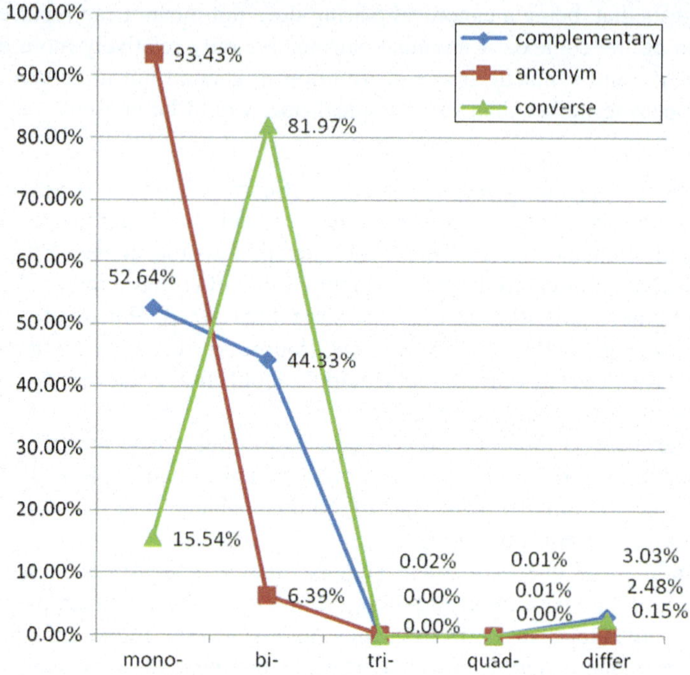

Fig. 4.10 Syllable distribution in Chinese opposite pairings

4.4.4 Syllable and Canonicity

For the ranking table of the 22 groups, we notice that all the top 5 candidate pairings are mono-syllabic or bi-syllabic. It suggests that, in Chinese, syllable may be a factor in defining the canonicity of being opposite pairing (Fig. 4.10).

As we can see in this figure for both complementary and antonym pairs, the most common pairings are mono-syllabic ones; but for converse pairs, the most common are bi-syllabic. 93.43% of antonym pairings are mono-syllabic, like 好: 坏 *hao3/good: huai4/bad*, 长: 短*chang2/long: duan4/short*, 轻: 重 *qing1/light: zhong4/heavy*; bi-syllabic ones only take 6.39%. Compared with that, 81.97% of converse pairings are bi-syllabic, like 买进: 卖出*mai3jin4/buy_in: mai4chu1/sell_out*, 教育: 学习 *jiao4yu4/teach: xue2xi2/learn*, 争取: 放弃 *zheng1que3/fight_for: fang4qi4/give_up*, and only 15.54% of this opposite category are mono-syllabic pairings. The distribution within the complementary category is more balanced. 52.64% of extracted sentences contain mono-syllabic pairings, and 44.33% of them contain bi-syllabic pairings. The percentages of tri-syllabic pairings and quad-syllabic pairings are very low in all the three categories. The highest percentage of tri-syllabic ones belongs to that of antonym, that is, 0.02%; and, quad-syllabic ones takes 0.01% in both antonym and converse groups, which are higher than that of complementary. Opposite pairings with different syllabic numbers, like 买: 卖出 *mai3/buy: mai4chu1/sell_out*, 前来: 去 *qian2lai2/come: qu4/go*, 胖: 苗条*pang4/obese: miao2tiao2/slim*, are relatively higher than these of tri- or quad-syllabic ones, but much lower than these of mono- or bi-syllabic ones. In our experiment, 3.03% of complementary pairings have different syllabic numbers, followed by 2.48% of antonym group and 0.15% of converse group. In this figure, complementary and antonym pairings show more similar trends than with converse.

Our data support the fact that an opposite pairing can be built with words having different numbers of syllables, but the ones with the same syllable number are dominant in usage. That is to say, the constructions of opposite pairing members are supposed to be the same.

4.5 Summary

In this chapter, we extend the study in Chap. 3 to the discourse level, in order to see: if collocated, what discourse function(s) do opposite pairs behave? Do canonical pairings exist for every conceptual opposite pair?

In order to answer the two questions, we design an experiment on Chinese opposite in discourse. 12 conceptual antonym pairs, 5 conceptual complementary pairs and 5 conceptual converse pairs are used to see their collocation hits in defined syntactic frames. In the end, 2,662 pairings extract 63,035 unique examples from the corpus, with a precision of around 90.03–93.55%.

The discourse function categorization of antonym shares with that of converse and complementary in discourse collocation. But the distribution of each function varies in the three sub-types of opposites in Chinese. Coordinated Opposite and Extreme Opposite are the top two frequent discourse functions for all the three Chinese opposite sub-types. And Numeric Opposite has a significant higher percentage in complementary than in the other two types. The basic tends of complementary, antonym and converse and similar to each; but, the distribution percentages, over different functions, of complementary and converse are closer, than compared with that of antonym.

We also compare our data of Chinese antonym with that of English and Japanese. The result shows that the discourse functions work well in Chinese data, and, there are differences among the three languages in discourse function distribution.

For the canonicity of being opposite, two factors—frequency and distribution of syntactic frames—are used to determine whether two conceptual opposite groups have canonical pairing(s). Generally speaking, the more frequent one pairing collocates, the wider distribution it has in syntactic frames. However, the two factors clash in some cases. It leads to the result that canonical pairing does exist in some conceptual opposite groups; while for others, it is hard to decide which one is the canonical one, or, none of the candidate pairings are dominant enough to be called the canonical pairing. Moreover, our data suggests, in Chinese, a relation exists between syllable number and being canonical. That is, pairing members with the same syllable number are much more frequent than the ones with different syllable numbers. And, for antonym and complementary groups, mono-syllabic pairings are more common; while for converse groups, bi-syllabic pairings are more common.

Chapter 5
Opposites and Negation

5.1 Research Question and Hypothesis

In Chap. 4, we discuss the experiment of Chinese opposite in discourse. In comparison with the ones from English and Japanese, our Chinese data shows that the negation patterns have a relatively lower percentage. The percentage of negation examples in Chinese is obviously less than the other discourse functions across all the three sub-types of opposites (0.28% in antonym, 0.04% in complementary, 0.02% in converse). And, the percentage of Chinese antonyms in negation patterns is also significantly less than that of English (2.07%) and Japanese (2.33%).

This is against the intuition of native language users. On the topic of opposites, negation is supposed to be the most involved pattern among others. Hence, in this chapter, we design a new experiment to trace how the negation patterns work in Chinese data. This is trying to answer the following questions: what kind(s) of pairing(s) would be triggered by negation patterns, such as "*shi4/be* a *bu4shi4/not_be* b", or, would any other semantic relations other than opposites be triggered out; and, if yes, what would be the distribution of these semantic relations. The results will help us to know why negation patterns have such a low percentage in the experiment of Chap. 4.

Before seeing the experiment result, our hypothesis is that: in the first place, these negation patterns would trigger some opposite pairings that are not listed in *Tongyici Cilin*; and, some parings may not be of opposite relation, but of other semantic relations, such as synonyms.

J. Ding, *A Lexical Semantic Study of Chinese Opposites*,
Frontiers in Chinese Linguistics 1, https://doi.org/10.1007/978-981-10-6184-4_5

5.2 Methodology, Candidate List and Corpus

In this experiment, we want to see what pairings would be triggered by negation patterns, so the triggering sentence is as follow:

a [negation pattern] b

Candidate words are placed in position a, and the triggered words in position b are recorded; then, candidate words are filled in position b and the triggered words in position a are recorded. By these two steps, we can see what words are used in negation patterns.

In order to keep consistent with our experiment in Chap. 4, we use the same negation patterns in this experiment. They are (Table 5.1).

For the same reason, the candidate list is the same one in Chap. 4. But this time, we do not have them separated under different concepts but combine them all in one single list (Table 5.2).

Besides, we still use GigaWord Corpora for this experiment. The segmentation of GigaWord helps us to avoid extracting information smaller or larger than the

Table 5.1 Negation frames

<table>
<tr><td>Negated opposite</td><td>宁愿A, (而|也|就) 不愿意 –A;
不但不 (是) A, 反而 (是) –A;
A不是|非 –A;
弘扬|颂扬|讴歌 A, 鞭挞|反对|抵制 –A;
避A就 –A;
verb A, 不verb –A (verb1 = verb2);</td></tr>
</table>

Table 5.2 Comparison of two candidate lists in experiments of opposite discourse function and negation

<table>
<tr><td>Candidate list of experiment in Chap. 4</td><td>Beautiful: 美|丽|俏|绮|妍|……姣好|秀美|秀气|……水灵灵|娇滴滴|曲线美|自然美|……千娇百媚|柔情绰态|娇艳欲滴|……
Ugly: 丑|陋|猥|……丑陋|难看|寒碜|猥琐|……其貌不扬|面目可憎|龇牙咧嘴|贼眉鼠眼|獐头鼠目|见不得人|人老珠黄|……
Even: 双|偶|对|复|俪|骈|……偶数|双数|对偶|双双|对仗|……
Come: 来|到|莅|至|临|……来到|到来|过来|……慕名而来|不期而至|翩然而至|乘兴而来|纷至沓来|……
……</td></tr>
<tr><td>Candidate list in position a/b in experiment of this chapter</td><td>美|丽|俏|绮|妍|……姣好|秀美|秀气|……水灵灵|娇滴滴|曲线美|自然美|……千娇百媚|柔情绰态|娇艳欲滴|……丑|陋|猥|……丑陋|难看|寒碜|猥琐|……其貌不扬|面目可憎|龇牙咧嘴|贼眉鼠眼|獐头鼠目|见不得人|人老珠黄|…… 双|偶|对|复|俪|骈|……偶数|双数|对偶|双双|……来|到|莅|至|临|……来到|到来|过来|……慕名而来|不期而至|翩然而至|乘兴而来|纷至沓来|……</td></tr>
</table>

word unit. But, because we do not establish restrictions for the semantic relation between words in position a and position b, any word may be triggered. It requires post-experiment checking to make sure of the accuracy of the extracted examples.

In the checking stage, we firstly rule out all the pairings which have only co-occurred once in the corpus. Since GigaWord is a very large corpus, such pairings are considered as randomly co-occurred ones and should be moved out.

Then, we manually check the rest of the sentences to remove the ones that are not semantically related, for example:

(103) 凭空[而]来

ping2kong1/depend_on_air [er2/but] lai2/come

"come out of nowhere"

Ping2kong1 is triggered by the pattern 'a 而 b', because it can combine with our candidate word *lai2* in the saying *ping2kong1er2lai2*. But *ping2kong1* itself does not have semantic relation with *lai2*, so this example is moved out of the result list.

(104) 中国大陆及欧亚美[非]大洋洲

zhong1guo2/China da4lu4/continent ji2/and ou1/Europe ya4/Asia mei3/America [fei1/Africa] da4yang2zhou1/Oceania

"China Mainland and the five continents?"

Mei3 in our candidate list means 'beauty' but the same character also means 'America', *fei1* is used as a negation pattern for its meaning of 'not' but the same character also means 'Africa', so Oceania is triggered by the unrelated meanings of *mei3* and *fei1*. This example should be removed too.

(105) 大型[非]制造业

da4xing2/large_scale fei1/not zhi4zao4ye4/industry

"large-scale non-industry"

There is a negation mark *fei1/not* in the middle of *da4xing2* and *zhi4zao4ye4/industry*, but *da4xing2/large_scale* is the modification of the phrase *fei1zhi4zao4ye4*, "non-industry". So it is not a good sentence of negation pattern with *fei1*.

(106) 有些事情是急[不]来的

you3xie1/some shi4qing2/issue shi4/BE ji2/rushing bu4lai2/not de0/DE

"some issues cannot be rushed"

Ji2bu4lai2 is an idiom, meaning "cannot be rushed". In it, *ji2/rushing* is the manner and *bu4lai2/not* is the complement for the manner. That is, *ji2* and *lai2* are not opposite pairing.

5.3 Result

For all the candidate words we have, 97 of them got 1169 valid results (Fig. 5.1).

The largest percentage (64.16%) of our data does not belong to the category of opposite, but to that of **sub-event**:

(107) 改进: 放弃

gai3jin4/improve: fang4qi4/give_up

我们只能改进不能放弃

wo3men0/we zhi3/only neng2/can gai3jin4/improve bu4/not neng2/can fang4qi4/give_up

"the only thing we can do is to improve but not give up the situation"

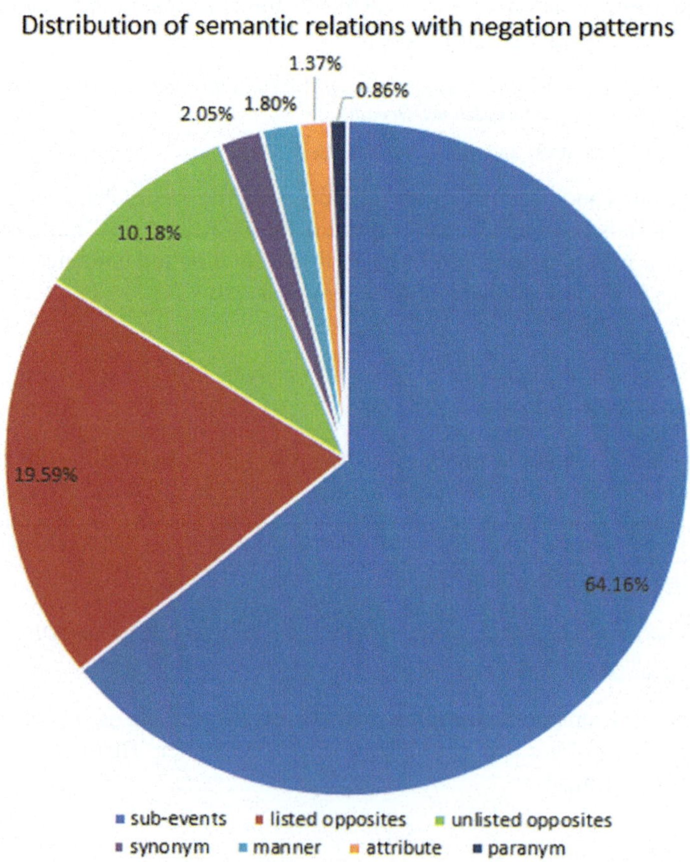

Fig. 5.1 Pie chart of distribution of semantic relations in negation pattern experiment

(108) 逛: 买

guang4/stroll: mai3/buy

只逛不买

zhi3/only guang4/stroll bu4/not mai3/buy

"window shopping"

(109) 贩卖: 赠送

fan4mai4/sell: zeng4song4/give_as_a_gift

这光碟只贩卖不赠送

zhe4/this guang1die2/CD zhi2/only fan4mai4/sell bu4/not zeng4song4/give_as_a_gift

"this CD is for sale only, it is not a free gift"

(110) 捡: 买

jian3/pick: mai3/buy

连队规定是捡不是买

lian2dui4/army gui1ding4/prescript shi4/BE jian3/pick bu4/not shi4/BE mai3/buy

"according to the army's regulations, (it should) use recycled stuff and not buy new ones"

The second largest percentage is taken by opposite pairs. 19.59% of the whole data are the opposite pairings which are listed in *Tongyici Cilin*, such as:

(111) 光明: 黑暗

guang1ming2/brightness: hei1an4/darkness

讴歌光明, 鞭笞黑暗

ou1ge2/eulogize guang1ming2/brightness, bian1chi4/flog hei1an4/darkness

"to eulogize the positive sides and flog the negative sides"

(112) 宽阔: 狭隘

kuan1kuo4/wide: xia2ai4/narrow

住在海岛的人心情是宽阔、不狭隘

zhu4/live zai4/at hai3/sea dao3/island de0/DE ren2/people xin1qing2/mind shi4/BE kuan1kuo4/wide, bu4/not xia2ai4/narrow

"the people living on islands have a broad, unlimited mind"

(113) 儿子: 女儿

er2zi0/son: nv3er0/daughter

其中三分之二是儿子, 不是女儿

qi2zhong1/among san1/three fen1/cut zhi1/DE er2/two shi4/BE er2zi0/son, bu4/not shi4/BE nv3er0/daughter

"two thirds of them are boys, not girls"

(114) 买进: 卖出

mai3jin4/buy: mai4chu1/sell

只买进不卖出

zhi2/only mai3jin4/buy bu4/not mai4chu1/sell

"only to buy not to sell"

And, 10.18% of the whole data are pairings which are opposites but are not listed in *Tongyici Cilin*. In the following examples, the first word is listed in *Tongyici Cilin* while the later one is not:

(115) 恶性: 良性

e4xing4/vicious: liang2xing4/beneficial

他希望是良性不是恶性竞争

ta1/he xi1wang4/hope shi4/BE liang2xing4/benefit bu4/not shi4/BE

"e4xing4/vicious jing4zheng1/competition"

(116) 雅: 俗

ya3/elegant: su2/vulgar

宜雅不宜俗

yi4/preferred ya3/elegant bu4/not yi4/preferred su2/vulgar

"(it is) preferred to be elegant not vulgar"

(117) 实事求是: 文过饰非

shi2shi4qiu3shi4/be_honest: wen2guo4shi4fei1/whitewash_mistakes

都要实事求是,不文过饰非

dou1/all yao4/need shi2shi4qiu3shi4/be_honest, bu4/not wen2guo4shi4fei1/whitewash_mistakes

"be honest with the fact, do not whitewash the mistakes"

(118) 空穴来风: 有凭有据

kong1xue4lai2feng1/groundless:you3ping2you3ju4/well-documented

柔性政变并非空穴来风, 是有凭有据

rou2xing3/flexible zheng4/politic bian4/change bing4fei1/not

kong1xue4lai2feng1/groundless, shi4/BE you3ping2you3ju4/well-documented

"the gradable politic revolution is not coming from nowhere but reasonable"

It proves that *Tongyici Cilin* does not include all the opposite pairings in Chinese. And, the negation patterns (and/or other semantic relation patterns) are helpful in finding out other opposite pairings by their co-occurrence in contexts.

2.05% of the extracted pairings are **synonyms** (or a restricted term of 'near-synonym'), for example:

(119) 胖: 壮

pang4/fat: zhuang4/sturdy

是胖不是壮

shi4/BE pang4/fat bu4/not shi4/BE zhuang4/sturdy

"(he/she) is fat not sturdy"

(120) 木讷: 专注

mu4ne4/rigid: zhuan1zhu4/concentrated

那目光是专注而不是木讷

na4/that mu4guang1/eye shi4/BE zhuan1zhu4/concentrated er2/but bu4/not shi4/BE mu4ne4/rigid

"those eyes are not rigid but concentrated"

(121) 优: 良

you1/excellent: liang2/well

几乎所有公务员都是不优即良

ji1hu1/almost suo3you3/all gong1wu4yuan2/civil_servant dou1/all shi4/BE bu4/not you1/excellent ji2/BE liang2/well

"the quality of each civil servant is at least not bad"

(122) 精明: 高明

jing1ming2/astute: gao1ming2/wise

要高明不要精明

yao4/want gao1ming2/wise bu4/not yao4/want jing1ming2/astute

"be wise not be astute"

According to Cruse (2006: 176), "a word is said to be a synonym of another word in the same language if one or more of its sense bears a sufficiently close similarity to one or more of the senses of the other word". The usage of negation patterns with these synonym pairings also agrees with Cruse, "synonyms will typically differ in respect of non-propositional aspects of meaning, such as expressive meaning and evoked meaning" (2006: 176). Such pairings sometimes are called near-synonyms, which "must share the same core meaning and must not have the primary function of contrasting with one another in their most typical contexts" (2006: 177). In the negation patterns, the differences between near-synonym pairing members are emphasized. Therefore it develops a feeling of contrasting within the pairing members, even if they share the same core meaning. We have a further discussion on negation and synonym relations in the next section of this chapter.

For the rest of the data, examples include **manners** (1.80%), such as:

(123) 快: 真

kuai4/fast: zhen1/real

求快不求真

qiu2/require kuai4/fast bu4/not qiu2/require zhen1/real

"to ensure a fast speed but not reality"

快: 好

kuai4/fast: hao3/good

魏京生只求快不求好

Wei4jing1sheng1/Wei_Jingsheng zhi3/only qiu2/require kuai4/fast bu4/not qiu2/require hao3/good

"what Wei Jingsheng needs is fast speed but not good quality"

(124) 精: 广

jing1/good_quality: guang3/wide_range

求精不求广

qiu2/require jing1/good_quality bu4/not qiu2/require guang3/wide_range

"to ensure a good quality but not wide range (of choice)"

精: 多

jing1/good_quality: duo1/large_quantity

贵精不贵多

gui4/attach_great_imporance_to jing1/good_quality bu4/not gui4/attach_great_imporance_to duo1/large_quantity

"to attach great importance to the quality but not quantity"

Attributes (1.37%), such as:

(125) 可靠: 耸人听闻

ke3kao4/reliable: song3ren2ting1wen2/sensational

报告是耸人听闻而不可靠的

bao4gao4/report shi4/BE song3ren2ting1wen2/sensational er2/and bu4/not ke3kao4/reliable de0/DE

"the report is sensational but not reliable"

(126) 聪明: 粗鲁

cong1ming2/clever: cu1lu3/rude

是极不聪明而粗鲁的做法

shi4/BE ji2/extremely bu4/not cong1ming2/clever er2/and cu1lu3/rude de0/DE zuo4fa3/action

"(it) is extremely un-clever and rude action"

(127) 灵活: 难

lin2huo3/flexible: nan2/difficult

试题整体看则不难而灵活

shi4ti2/test_question zheng3ti3/whole kan4/look ze2/BE bu4/not nan2/difficult er2/and lin2huo2/flexible

"the character of whole test is not difficult but flexible"

Paranymy is a new term defined only in recent years. It is "a relation between any two lexical items belonging to the same semantic classification" (Huang et al. 2007: 2). The two basic requirements for being paranymy relations are: "paranyms are a type of coordinate term, since they share the same hypernym", and, "paranyms have to share the same classificatory criteria" (2007: 2). In our data, examples of paranyms (0.86%) include:

(128) 神: 人

shen2/god: ren2/people

法官是人, 不是神

fa3guan1/judger shi4/BE ren2/people, bu4/not shi4/BE shen2/god

"judger is common people, not god"

(129) 金钱: 理想

jin1qian2/money: li3xiang3/ideal

只讲金钱, 不讲理想

zhi3/only jiang3/consider jin1qian2/money, bu4/not jiang3/consider li3xiang3/ideal

"to chase money only rather than ideal"

(130) 教育: 科技

jiao4yu4/education: ke1ji4/technology

中国大陆重科技, 不重教育

zhong1guo2/China da4lu4/mainland zhong4/focus_on ke1ji4/technology, bu4/not zhong4/focus_on jiao4yu4/education

"China Mainland pays a lot of attention to technology rather than education"

教育: 商业

jiao4yu4/education: shang1ye4/commercial

游学是商业行为, 不是教育行为

you2xue2/studying_trip shi4/BE shang1ye4/commercial xing2wei2/action, bu4/not shi4/BE jiao4yu4/education xing2wei2/action

"studying trip is commercial rather than educational action"

教育: 劳役

jiao4yu4/education: lao2yi4/servitude

政府对于少年犯应给予的是教育, 而不是劳役

zheng4fu3/government dui4yu2/to shao4nian2/youngster fan4/delinquent ying1/should ji1yu3/give de0/DE shi4/BE jiao4yu4/education, er2/but bu4/not shi4/BE lao2yi4/servitude

"government should offer education but not servitude to juvenile delinquents".

5.4 Discussion

Using the negation patterns, we can construct a binary relation between the position a and b. The result of triggered pairings shows that such a binary relation is applied wider than only opposites in Chinese data. Such a result agrees with our hypothesis. Then, why would other semantic relations, like synonyms or paranyms, be involved in negation patterns? Is negation in logic the (formal) definition of opposites in languages? And, is the opposite, or any of its sub-types, a binary relation?

5.4.1 *Negation in Classical Logic and in Languages*

As it is pointed out by Ding and Huang (2012), logic negation does not always work the same in language. In Classic Logic, for a certain domain α, for the pair of A and B, if:

$$A = \bar{B}, B = \bar{A}$$

and, $A \cup B, A \cap B = \phi$

So, the negation of A goes to B, and the negation of B goes to A;

It is also noted that, Aristotle distinguishes contrary from contradictory in logics: "the negation of one predication entails its contradictory", like *true: false*, *red: not red*; at the same time, "the assertion of one predicate entails the denial of its contrary, but in which both contraries may be false", like *red: green*, *big: small* (Lehrer and Lehrer 1982). Later, in Lyons' (1977) work, it is how the distinction of "ungradable and gradable lexemes within the class of opposites in a language" is made. Furthermore, he notes that, gradability causes that fact that "gradable antonyms[1] can generally be taken as contraries". Similar discussions can also be found in other theorists' work (Cruse 1986; Lyons 1977; Mettinger 1994, among others).

Ding and Huang conclude, such discussions show that, in theoretical talk, the definition of opposite are using the ones of logical negation but the two of them are

[1]"Gradable antonym" in Lyons's term is the same to that of "antonym" in our paper. To avoid confusion, readers can go back to Sect. 1.3, Basic Terms, for the definitions.

not exactly the same. In fact, in languages, opposite pairing members do not necessarily follow the logical negation rules.

A Negation Test

(a) (complementary) 死: 活 (*si3/dead: huo2/alive*)

For the statement of 小明死了 ("Xiao-ming is dead"), the negation of it is 小明没死 ("Xiao-ming is not dead"), which is equal to 小明活着 ("Xiao-ming is alive"). Reversely, for the statement of 小明活着 ("Xiao-ming is alive"), the negated one is 小明没活着 ("Xiao-ming is not alive"). Hence, for the pair of *si3: hou2*, the negation of one goes to the other of the pair. In other words, when *Xiao-ming is dead* is negated, and then it should mean that *Xiao-ming is (still) alive*. Meanwhile, the negation of *Xiao-ming is alive* only implies the one that *Xiao-ming is dead*. However, in real language using, it is also natural to have the phrases like 半死不活 *ban4/half si3/dead bu4/not huo2/alive* "half dead half alive", which means still alive but exhausted of energy. The negation of *huo2* in this phrase does not have the equal meaning of *si3*, because in such case the complementary opposite of *si3: hou2*is gradable, a concept which will be explained in later section of this chapter.

(b) (antonym) 高兴: 伤心 (*gao1xing4/happy: shang1xin1/sad*)

For statements like 她高兴 ("she is happy"), the negated one is 她不高兴 ("she is not happy"), which might be understood as "she is sad", "she is angry" or "she is emotionless now". "She is not happy" does not need to be "she is sad". Reversely, the negation of 她伤心 ("she is sad") is not necessarily equal to "she is happy". Negation test fails to work in antonym pairs.

(c) (converse) 买: 卖 (*mai3/buy: mai4/sell*)

For the statement 张三买了一辆车 ("Zhang-san brought a car"), the negation of it is 张三没有买一辆车 ("Zhang-san did not bring a car"), which does not equal to "Zhang-san sold a car". The negation of the member of this pair does not have only one understanding. So, again, the negation test fails in the pair of *mai3: mai4*.

Hence in natural languages, like Chinese, a purely logical definition of negation fails to work in many cases. Only for complementary pairs, the domain where they apply to is divided into two parts which combine the whole domain but mutually exclusive, so the negation of one member always goes to the opposite one. But for antonym and converse pairs, the negation test fails.

So far, Ding and Huang have proved that, 'negator + seed word' does not necessary equal to the opposite of the seed word in meaning. That is to say, logical negation cannot be used as the (formal) definition for opposite in language, at least not for all the opposite pairings. The part(s) which is/are negated in negation pattern varies, according to the semantic relation between two positions in the negation pattern.

5.4.2 Semantic Relations in Negation Frames

"STOP HERE": Sub-events in Negation Frames

For the cases like 逛 *guang4/stroll*: 买 *mai3/buy* the event structure is a better explanation of their co-occurrence in negation frames. In the event of shopping, the customer needs to experience the processing like: knowing what he or she needs to buy, searching for the thing(s) in the shop (or, in an online shop, in modern days), then buying it. In the case of 只逛不买 *zhi3guang4bu4mai3*, "window shopping", the negator (不 *bu4/not*) negates the following event (*mai3/buy*) after *guang4/stroll*, so the processing of shopping stops at the stage of searching, and does not go on to the step of paying for something. In such cases, the negation is making a stop between the sub-event which happens, and the one which is expected to happen.

In such cases, if given enough context information, the later part of negation pattern might be deleted and yet the meaning stays the same. For example, (shopkeeper): 您需要什么吗?

ning2/you xu1yao4/need shen2me0/what ma0/MA?

"Can I help you?"

(passerby): 我只看看 (不买东西)
wo3/I zhi3/only kan4kan4/look-look (bu4/not mai3/buy dong1xi0/issue)

"Just have a look (not buy anything)."

In the context of shopping or trading, the former part is enough to express the meaning that "I am not going to buy anything" and for the aspect of euphemism it is not necessary to finish the later part.

Fully Negated Cases: Opposites in Negation Frames

In our data, 19.59% of examples have position a and b filled by an opposite pairing. In Sect. 2.3, in the experiment on four-syllabic compounds, there are similar cases like 聚少离多 *jv4/get_together shao3/less li2/depart duo1/more* "more departed than gottogether", 否极泰来 *pi3/bad_luck ji2/end tai4/good_luck lai2/come* "bad luck ends and good luck succeeds", 优胜劣汰 *you1/good sheng4/win lie4/bad tai4/eliminate* "survival of the best". These are combined by two opposite pairings, in the form of [A1][A2][−A1][−A2]. The meaning of [A1][A2] is equal to that of [−A1][−A2], and together they double emphasize the same meaning. Here, the combination of one negation pattern with one opposite pairing can be seen as the form of [A1][A2][−A1][−A2] extended to a larger context.

In these cases, either of the two parts of negation patterns, for example, the part of *xin1qing2/mind shi4/BE kuan1kuo4/wide* and the part of *(xin1qing2/mind shi4/BE) bu4/not xia2ai4/narrow,* can be deleted while the sentence will still be understood correctly, since the meanings of two parts overlap.

Besides, we notice that, in the 19.59% of examples, most of them are triggered by negators like 不 *bu4/not*, 没 *mei3/not*, 非 *fei1/not*, 反 *fan3/against* and so on. Such words are also called negative prefixes in Chinese studies. Since Chinese words are combined by characters, the suffixes usually also take one character position, and that will make the derived one more likely to be treated as a compound or even a phrase, which is considered to be less likely to combine a pair with the stem word. For example, 好 *hao3/good:* 不好 *bu4hao3/not_good* (or, 坏 *huai4/bad*). The word *bu4hao3* negates the semantic meaning of *hao3* in a wider scale than by only asserting *huai4*; but our intuition, if we are right with most of the native Chinese speakers, would probably prefer to take *huai4*, rather than *bu4hao3*, as the opposite pairing members for *hao3*. It is probably because that *huai4* is more syllabic matched with *hao3* rather than *bu4hao3*, as we have proved in our last study, in Chap. 4. Besides, only very few Chinese words take the derivational morphemes within the new characters. The most common example is 歪, *wai1/not_upright*. The upper radical of it is 不, *bu4/not,* and the bottom radical is 正, *zheng4/upright* and the whole meaning of *wai1* is almost the same as 不正, *bu4/not zheng4/upright.* But this kind of morphology is very rare in Chinese. Hence, for most cases in Chinese, the stem words and the derived ones with a negative suffix would probably not be considered as an opposite pair in the morphological aspect.

Synonyms as Opposites: Synonyms in Negation Frames

In the test, the synonyms—although not taking a large percentage—co-occurs with negation frames. Synonyms, or strictly near-synonyms, deal with the relation of the two words "involving sameness of sense", or "if they are mutually hyponymous" (Cann 2011: 458). On the other hand, the presupposition of being an opposite pair is that the two words have to share the sameness in (probably) all the aspects but the one where they contrast. Hence, both synonym pairs and opposite pairs can be seen as members sharing the sameness while differing in some aspects.

So, how can a language user naturally find that the relation between *big: small* is oppositeness, but the one between *big: large* more like synonymy? Or, how can we distinguish opposites from synonyms?

A possible answer is that the pairs of opposites and synonyms share different focuses; for opposites, it is the differences of the pair members that speakers focus on; and for synonyms, it is the similarities.

It is called "simultaneous closeness" by Cruse (1986: 197), that the all the features of an opposite pair are similar or identical, except the one dimension of meaning where they are different from each. And it is along the dimension of difference, the pair occupies opposing poles.

On the other hand, Palmer (1981: 88) suggests that languages like English are particularly rich in synonyms, since its vocabulary origins are from different resources, like Anglo-Saxon, French, Latin and Greek. That explains why there are so many synonyms for some entries in the dictionary and online thesauruses. Opposites, although regular and natural in languages, are of relatively smaller size, at least for English. As we can see from *Tongyici Cilin*, for the 44 conceptual groups we chose, the average size of each synonym group is 54.07 words; within these groups, 2663 valid opposite parings are found in the corpus, hence for the average pairing number for every opposite conceptual pair is 121.05, and the average opposite number for each word is 2.24. That is to say, for every word in our candidate list, it has 53.07 words as synonyms while only 2.24 words as opposites. This result matches the above general hypothesis. Also, since the synonym group size is so big, it is necessary to point out the variations between synonyms. And that suggests why synonyms can also co-occur in negation patterns.

In the negation experiment, the distinct between *pang4* and *zhuang4* is more like the ones of **conceptual meaning** (or, **logical meaning**) and **connotative meaning** (Leech 1981). "Connotative meaning is the communicative value an expression has by virtue of what it refers to, over and above its purely conceptual content." The conceptual meaning of *pang4* and *zhuang4* are the same. That is, they both refer to something oversized (in semantic features, +size +oversized), but the connotative meaning of *pang4* (+unfitting) is more negative than *zhuang4* (+healthy). Moreover, the nouns collocate with *pang4* or *zhuang4* are not the same, which is called (**collocative meaning**):

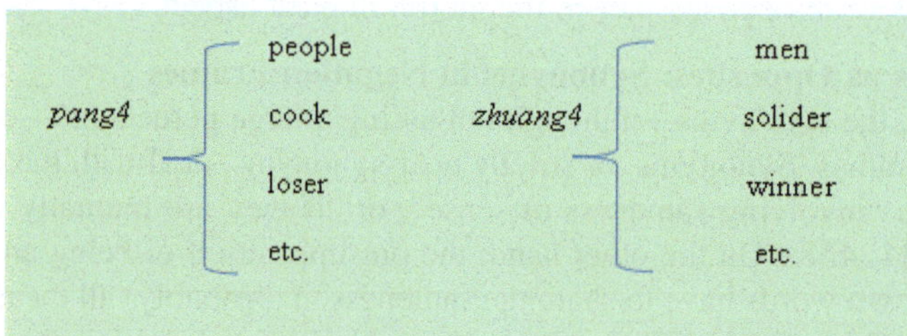

And, such a difference results in different **affective meanings**. When the speaker uses *pang4* to describe someone, he or she is at the same time expressing the unspoken but implied emotion like antipathy; while for *zhuang4*, it suggests the emotions like admiration or appreciation.

As Leech points out, connotative meaning and conceptual meaning are overlapping in a large extent. However, the usage of negation pattern is to distinguish the un-overlapped part(s) of two words, which are sharing the same semantic features. In other words, the negation pattern is highlighting the semantic feature(s) of later words, which is distinct from the former one, by negating the former word. Actually it is only negating the distinctive feature(s) of former word. At the same time, the negation pattern also doubly affirms the basic meaning or conceptual meaning. Since it stays the same through the pattern(s), it is used as the unmarked semantic feature for understanding. For example, in sentence:

(131) 是胖不是壮

shi4/BE pang4/fat bu4/not shi4/BE zhuang4/sturdy

"(he/she) is fat not sturdy" (Fig. 5.2).

胖 *pang4/fat* is affirmed and 壮 *zhuang4/sturdy* is negated. But it is not the whole meaning of *zhuang4* is negated. It is only the connotative meaning,

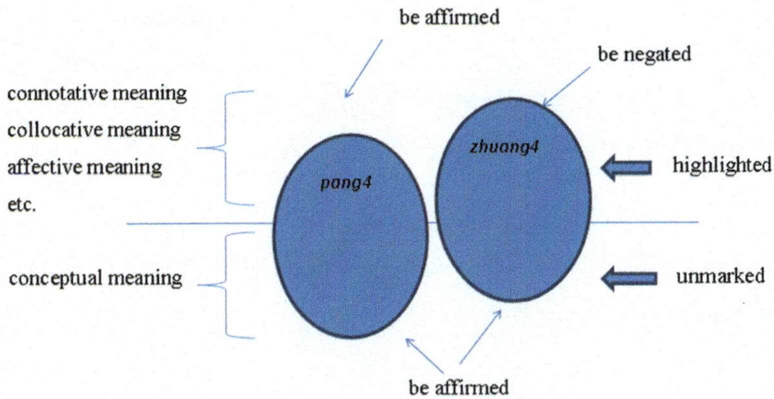

Fig. 5.2 Explanation of synonyms *pang4: zhuang4* in negation frame

collocative meaning and affective meaning of *zhuang4*, where the two words differ, are negated. Meanwhile, the meaning shared by *zhuang4* and *pang4*, that is, the conceptual meaning, is affirmed as the unmarked meaning. The negation frame is used here to highlight the un-overlapped parts of *pang4* and *zhuang4*.

In the paper *Semantic networks of English*, Miller and Fellbaum (1991) write for synonymy and opposite ('antonymy' is the term they use): '... the ability to judge that relation [synonymy] is a prerequisite for the representation of meanings in a lexical matrix. According to one definition (usually attributed to Leibniz) two expressions are synonymous if the substitution of one for the other never changes the truth value of a sentence in which the substitution is made.' (1992: 202). Such a definition of synonymy is somehow clear enough to be made; however, for the one of opposite, they note that "antonymy, which turns out to be surprisely difficult to define. The antonym of a word *x* is sometimes *not-x*, but not always... Antonymy, which seems such a simple symmetrical relation, is at least as complex as the other semantic relations, yet speakers of English have no trouble recognizing antonyms when they see them."(1992: 203). But as least they are right about one thing: opposite, as with the other semantic relations, is a symmetrical relation.

According to the definitions given by previous literature, we can generalize the principles of being (restricted) opposites:

The pairing of language unit A and language unit B can be called opposite, if and only if they,

1. Are under the same domain;
2. Contrast in only one aspect, but are the same in all the rest;
3. The extension of A is equal to the intension of B, and vice versa.

Above is a purely logical definition for opposite, that is to say, only the logically restricted opposite pairings can satisfy these conditions. Hence, the best examples of such opposite pairings are the complementary ones. Besides, the ones combined by unmarked and marked words are also always restricted opposites, such like,

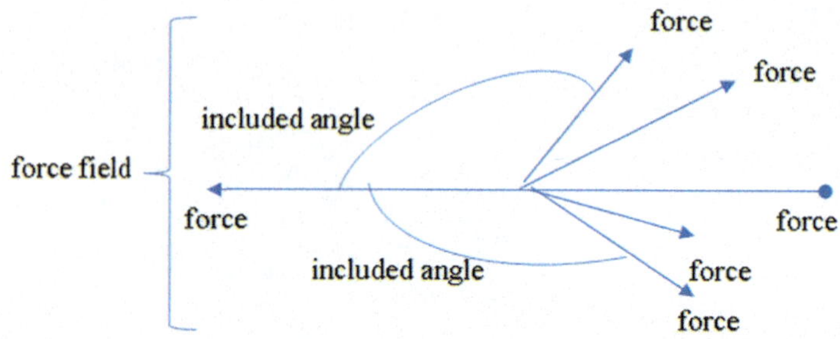

Fig. 5.3 Force field

happy: unhappy, *legal: illegal*; sometimes, it would also be the cases of one word versus one phrase, like *long: not long.*[2]

We also generalize the principles of being (in general) synonym.

The pairing of language unit A and language unit B can be called synonyms, if and only if they,

1. Are under the same domain;
2. The same in most aspects, but, different (the extent may vary in cases) in at least one aspect.

Rule 2 in both principles for opposite and synonym make the foundation of synonym pairings become opposite pairings in certain situation(s). Let's use a very basic mechanical figure to explain (Fig. 5.3).[3]

Hence, the closer the included angle is to 180° (that is, to be a straight angle), the more likely the two members are considered to be an opposite pairing, rather than synonym pairing (Fig. 5.4).

(Force field = the domain where the relation lay in

Point of force application = the aspect where the two members vary from each

Included angle = the extent of how they differ from each)

Now, we can see that Rule 3 for the principles of being an (restricted) opposite is actually one additional remark for Rule 2. Then, we modify the previous principles to the following new ones:

[2]It is interesting to notice that, the lexicalized opposite pairings are usually the ones of taxonomy, while as to the ones of antonym, it is harder to find the lexicalized words in both sides; moreover, for converse, it is even harder to have both sides occupied by lexicalized words, for example, **buy: not buy*. On the other hand, it means, in reverse, there are more lexicalized words in both sides for antonym and converse in a less restricted extent, for example, *long: short*, and *buy: sell*.

[3]We now only explain the situation between two members, so a two-dimensional field is enough. For the situation of more than two members, an according higher-dimensional space is necessary. In this paper, we mainly use two member pairings as examples, because of the practical consideration of paper writing; but the higher world is full of possibilities, so we leave it to later studies.

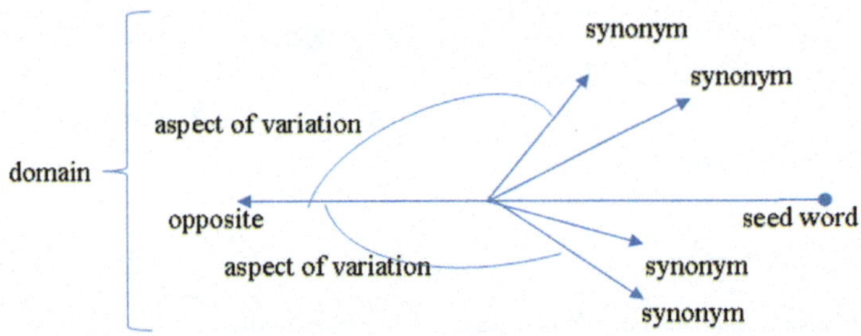

Fig. 5.4 Synonyms and opposites in a certain domain

The pairing of language unit A and language unit B can be called opposite, if and only if they,

1. Are under the same domain;
2. Are the same in all aspects, except one, in which **the extension of A (in this aspect) is equal to the intension of B (in the same aspect)**, and vice versa.

That explains, in theory, why synonym pairings can become opposite ones.

This assessment might seem to be too rough. We need to have a close exploration with some more situations before safely arriving at it: why some pairings are more easily treated as opposite pairings than others?

We may recall that in the experiment on Chinese fixed words (see Chap. 2), there are some cases like 前仰后合, *qian2yang3hou4he2*, "stagger forward and back", which are termed as [A][S][−A][S]. From historical point, however, such a saying is arguable. Because *yang3*, "falling backward" and *he2*, "falling forward", have opposite moving directions, in ancient Chinese, and are used to be a kind of opposite. That is also why *yang3* can only be aligned to *qian2* (forward), and *he2* to *hou3* (backward), as the directional words naturally selected by the verbs' meanings. But now in modern Chinese, they are more used as synonyms to laymen. *Qian2yang3hou4he2* is one of the many cases of how opposites in ancient Chinese generally become near-synonyms in modern Chinese. By that, it is suggested that the gap between opposites might not be as huge as we thought. The terms "opposite" or "synonym" should be pragmatic ones, but not (or at least not only) semantic ones. The crucial factor to becoming a synonym or opposite might be decided by the semantic focus of the utterance. Once the focus is placed on the difference of the two words, they are more used as opposite; when the focus is on the (unmarked) similarity of the two, they are more used as synonyms.

Make a Choice: Manner, Attribute and Paranym in Negation Frames

Manners in Negation Frames

Let's take the group of 快 *kuai4/fast* for example. In the saying 求快不求真 qiu2/contrast of *kuai4/fast* and *zhen1/real*, *kuai4* is used in the measurement of speed but *zhen1* is used for the reality; similarly, *hao3/good* is for the quality. That

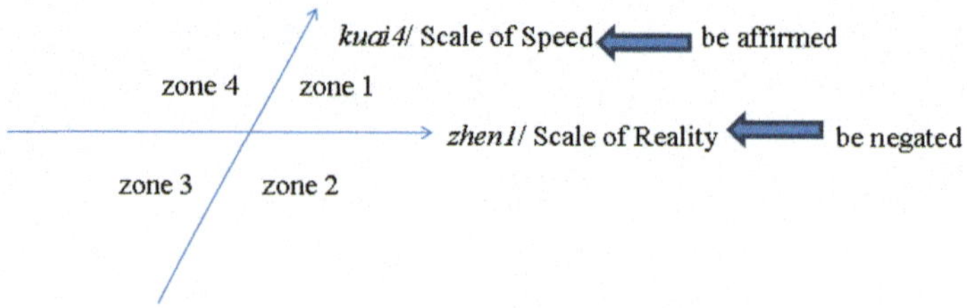

Fig. 5.5 Explanation of manners *kuai4: zhen1* in negation frame

means, the negation pattern is constructed on two kinds of measurement scales (Fig. 5.5).

In this example, the scale of speed is affirmed while the one of reality is negated. So, what is wanted by this phrase is either zone 1 (fast and real) or zone 4 (fast but not real). They are both advantaged in the scale of speed, but not necessarily advantaged in the scale of reality. On the other hand, the advantage of zone 2 in reality does not make it chosen by this pattern; zone 3 (not real nor fast) is not wanted, either. In fact, the implied meaning of this saying should be "being hurry to complete something at the price of the reality/quality". Hence, the negation between manners expresses the chosen among different manner scales.

Attributes in Negation Frames

There are three forms of negation with the category of attributes.

In sentence (132):

(132) 报告是耸人听闻而不可靠的

bao4gao4/report shi4/BE song3ren2ting1wen2/sensational er2/and bu4/not ke3kao4/reliable de0/DE

"the report is sensational but not reliable"

耸人听闻 *song3ren2ting1wen2/sensational* is the reason of being unreliable (*bu4/not ke3kao4/reliable*). Because the report uses outrageous statements to cover the fact, it is not reliable to readers (Fig. 5.6).

In sentence (133):

(133) 是极不聪明而粗鲁的做法

shi4/BE ji2/extremely bu4/not cong1ming2/clever er2/and cu1lu3/rude de0/DE zuo4fa3/action

"(it) is extremely un-clever and rude action"

粗鲁 *cu1lu3/rude* is a euphemism for being stupid, or, bu4 *cong1ming2*, "not clever".

For some reason, it is unlikely to have the statement of "it is a stupid action", so it uses a negation with the modifier*ji2/extremely* to imply the opposite meaning of "clever". At the same time, cu1lu3 does not only mean "rude" but also is projecting to the point of "being (Fig. 5.7).

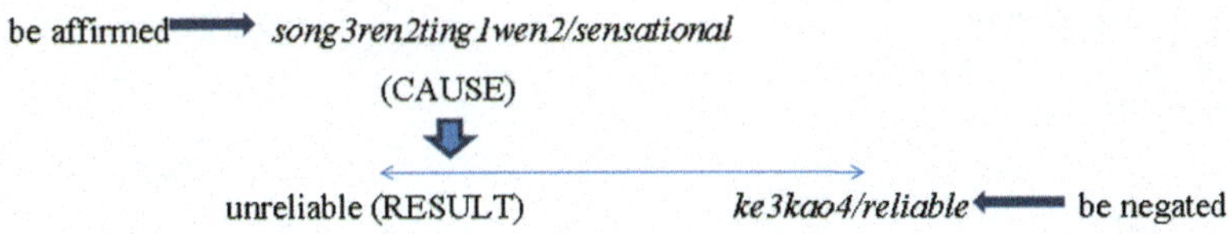

Fig. 5.6 Explanation of attributes *song3ren2ting1wen2: ke3kao4* in negation frame

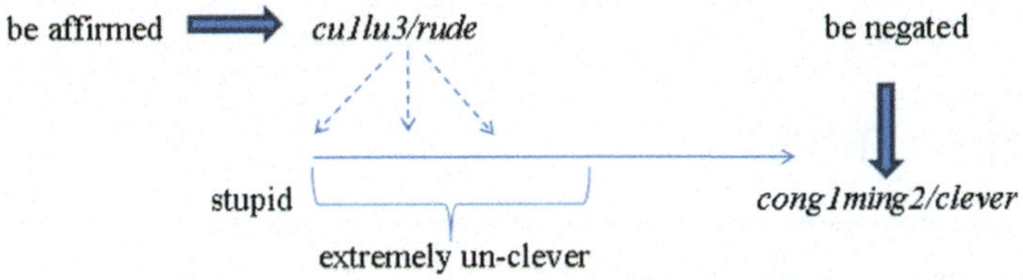

Fig. 5.7 Explanation of attributes *cu1lu3: cong1ming2* in negation frame

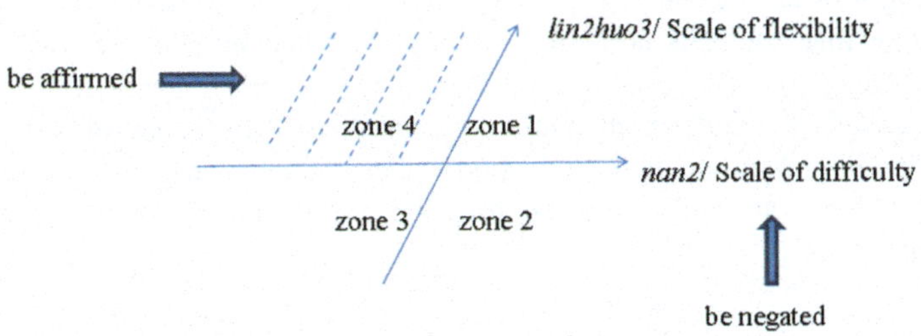

Fig. 5.8 Explanation of attributes *lin2huo3: nan2* in negation frame

In sentence (134):

(134) 试题整体看则不难而灵活

shi4ti2/test_question zheng3ti3/whole kan4/look ze2/BE bu4/not nan2/difficult er2/and lin2huo2/flexible

"the character of whole test is not difficult but flexible"

Its model is similar to that of *qiu2 kuai4 bu4 qiu2 zhen1* (in the case of manners). But, in this sentence (134), only zone 4 (not difficult but flexible) is chosen (Fig. 5.8).

Paranyms in Negation Pattern

Paranyms are the ones sharing the same hypernym in ontology network. "Cat" and "dog" are paranyms since they are all under the category of animal. The usage of negation frames with paranyms is similar to that of synonyms. However, in some sentences like:

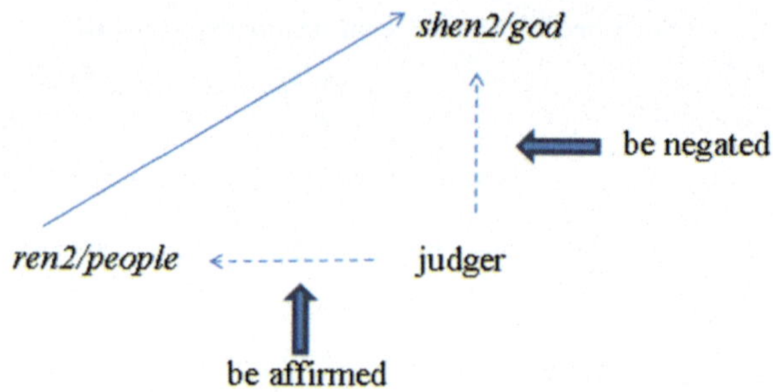

Fig. 5.9 Explanation of paranyms *ren2: shen2* in negation frame

(135) 法官是人, 不是神

fa3guan1/judger shi4/BE ren2/people, bu4/not shi4/BE shen2/god

"judger is common people, not god"

The negation frame is constructing a contrast between 人 *ren2/people* and 神 *shen2/god*, and also building a rank to imply that one of them ("god") is hierarchically higher than the other ("people"). By doing so, the sentence is suggesting the meaning that "there is something cannot be done by a judger (as a common people)" (Fig. 5.9).

In the cases of manners, attributes and paranyms, the negation frame must be used completely. Neither of the two parts (the negated one and the affirmed one) can be omitted. Otherwise, the meaning of the sentence cannot be understood completely.

5.4.3 *Negation as a Binary Relation?*

In Ding and Huang (2013), the negation test successes on the complementary and converse pairs and, at the same time, fails to work on gradable antonym pairs such as *happy: sad*. Such a result brings a new question: is the negation relation a binary or multiple?

For some subtypes of opposition, like complementaries, the two members of the pair dichotomize the related domain; while some others, like in the gradable antonym, the domain contains more than two members which may be said to have meaning contrasts, along certain scales or dimensions. That is to say, for a normal circumstance, someone that is not *alive* should be *dead*, but the utterance of someone being *happy* is not equal to that of someone being *sad*. So in the later example, other kinds of emotions can be used instead of being sad, to contrast with being happy, or, equal to being not happy.

Even for the complementary pairs, it is necessary to identify the related domain this pair is applied to, in order to have the negation and double-negation rules work.

A table or a chair, for example, is not applicable for the pair of *die: alive* (cf. e.g., Lyones 1977).

Also, in natural language use, it is not rare to have the complementary pairs—very often is one member of the pair—coerced into being gradable. Again, let's take *die: alive* for example.

Cruse (1986) concludes that some complementary adjectives are not normally gradable, but points out that very often one member of a pair is more likely to be grading than the other, like: ?*very dead*, ?*moderately dead*, ?*deader than before*; but, *very alive*, *moderately alive*, *more alive than before*.

And, Murphy (2011) agrees that "complementaries can sometimes be used as contraries, and contraries sometimes are used as complementaries", even for some gradable pairs, "the denial of one is usually taken to be the assertion of the other" [9], like *Ari is not honest* normally entails *Ari is dishonest*, and vice versa. Actually, according to Cruse (1986), this problem is solved by "maintaining that such words must have two senses, one in complementary opposition and the other in contrary opposition to its antonym".

Pairs like *buy: sell* offers another aspect of looking at the binarity of being opposites. In the normal trading domain, there are, usually, only the contrast of buying and selling. Their meanings are converse because: for any *X* buys *Y* from *Z*, then it is true that, *Z* sells *Y* to *X*. However, the two-member-relation is not necessary enough to generate the implication like complementary pairs in the negation and double-negation tests. That is because, logically speaking, if *X* is not buying *Y*, then it is not to say *X* is selling *Y*—it is also even possible for *X* to do nothing with *Y*. The two-member-relation between *buy* and *sell* is coinciding with the human tendency to categorize experience in terms of binary contrasts, as linguists (Cruse 1986; Cann 2011; Murphy 2011) pointed out.

From the negation and double-negation tests, we can see that, within one sentence, binary relations fail in many cases with opposite pairings. In fact, the possibility within the grey area between the pairings, or multiple relations they have, leads the negation patterns to trigger out different results.

For a complementary pair of *dead* and *alive*, the result might show that they are the same as the logical negation and double-negation assumptions. Because in the domain they are applied to, the pairs of complementary "exhaustively divide some conceptual domain into two mutually exclusive compartments" (Cruse 1986: 198). The example of *dead: alive* is expressed as someone must be alive or dead at a given time, and there is no middle statement between the pair—either X or non-X must be asserted in this situation and the other must be negated at the same time. Actually in Chinese, however, we have the saying 半死不活 *ban4/half si3/dead bu4/not huo2/alive*, which should be literally translated to "half-dead-not-alive", and in fact refers to the state of *being half-dead* in English. So in saying it, the speaker is willing to describe a state that a man is still alive biologically but nearly dead, because of the exhaustion of energy. It is also pointed out by Cruse, who notes that "complementarity… is to some extent a matter of degree" (1986: 200). So for the ghosts and vampires, it is hard to say whether they are alive or dead (Cruse 1986).

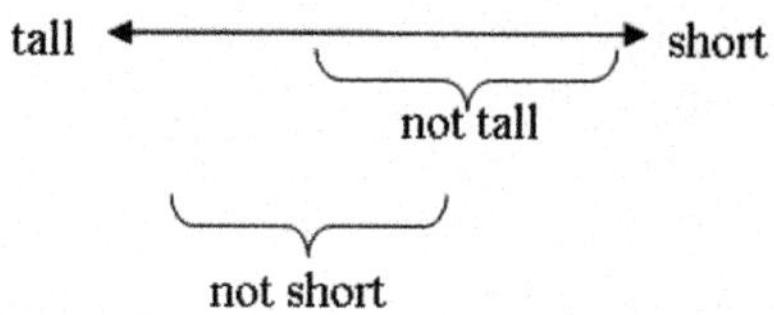

Fig. 5.10 Negations of *tall: short*

Cann also notes that the binary antonyms can be easily coerced into being gradable, if the conceptual domain which is bisected by the pair disappears. That, he thinks, explains why we can say someone is not very *alive* without committing that he or she is very *dead* (cf. Cann 2011).

For the pairs of **antonyms**, we have examples of *tall: short* and *happy: sad*. The results for these two pairs are not the same. When the utterance of someone being tall is negated, it is possible for the speaker to say that he or she is short or of medium height. When double-negating the statement of being tall, it is probable to say that someone is tall, or someone is tall but not as tall as he is supposed to be. In any case, the results of negation and double-negation of being tall or short moves along the axis of height (Fig. 5.10).

But, to the pair of *happy: sad*, it seems that the negations of either side might not necessarily go to the other one, nor the double-negations go back to the original side. Taking *happy* as the starting point, the negation of happy can go to diverse directions in the picture. The statement of being *sad* is only one of these possibilities where the negation of *happy* may refer to. The negation of *happy* can also trigger out emotions like *depressed*, *angry* and so on.

Also, the negation of someone is being sad does not necessarily refer to he or she being happy, but also that being *excited*, *hopeful*, *comforting*, *loved* and so on.

That also explains why the diversion of double-negation of being *happy* may not go back to be *happy*:

$$\text{happy} \rightarrow \text{sad} \rightarrow \text{comforting} \rightarrow \cdots$$

Cruse (1986: 197) points out that the opposite relation we feel in pairs like *happy: sad* is probably the most salient and deeply felt of all lexical relations and most likely to be gained at a very young age. Cruse points out that the direct lexical recognition of opposites is received in everyday language using. So even children are capable to answer the questions like "what is the opposite of XX" (Cruse 2004).

However, in response to the criteria we have mentioned to distinct oppositeness from synonymy, it is also arguable to say the relation between *happy: sad* is oppositeness or two frequently-used positive and negative mentions. The later relation is not as same as oppositeness, although they may look similar. Because there are many other emotions or statements such as *being excited*, *hopeful*, *comforting*, *angry*, *quiet* and so on, *being happy* is not the presupposition of *being sad* and neither is the reverse. Of course, the two are undoubtedly respectively standing at two polarities of positive and negative scales. Besides, they are probably the most frequently used emotion words. Hence, they are usually treated as an opposite pair.

Fig. 5.11 Negation and double negation of *happy*

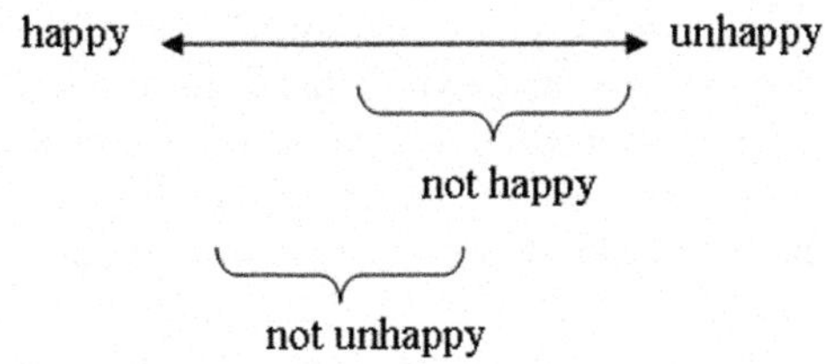

But the above picture and analysis have already illustrated that it is some kind problematic to define their opposite relation.

It is not to say that emotion words do not have opposite(s). For the word *happy*, a better opposite member might be *unhappy*, rather than *sad* or *angry*. At a first glance, it is possible to say *happy: unhappy* a complementary pair. But the fact is their negation and double negation results are similar to the ones of *tall: short*: the negation of one does not arrive at the other, neither does the double-negation go back to the starting member, though the movements keep along the same axis (Fig. 5.11).

For the discussion on happy, we stop here but a more detailed exploration of negation and double-negation for the pair *happy: unhappy* can be found in Manfred (2007).

For a **converse** pair like *buy: sell*, we find that the negation of one member does not always go to the other, but the double-negation of one goes back.

Lyons (1977) treats such pairs as "three-place predicates and correlate the order of the terms in the symbolic representation of the relations R(x, y, z)", so the relation of *buy* and *sell* can be transposed by 'buy' (x, y, z) = 'sell' (z, y, x). The pair of *husband: wife* is treated as "two-place predicates", so husband (x, y) = wife (y, x). (Lyons 1977: 280) Later, Curse also describes converses as "two-place if the relational predicate they denote has two arguments", like *above: below*, "three-place if it has three", like *lend: borrow* and "arguably four-place converses", like *sell: buy* (Cruse 2004: 167).

We can have the three pairs mentioned above illustrated as following:

husband (x, y) = wife (y, x): husband ———— wife

lend (x, y, z) = borrow (z, y, x): lend ———— borrow

object ----------->

buy (x, y, m, z) = sell (z, m, y, x): buyer ———— seller

<---------- good

money --------->

Lyons (1977) marks that it is a universal human tendency to "dichotomize or polarize our judgments and experiences", so there is no wonder why all the examples of opposites (at least in his book) have in common that they depend on dichotomization.

However, as we have seen above, the opposite pairs may also generate from relations such as incompatibility and contrast. Such relations, sometimes, contain more than only two members. Lehrer's semantic field theory arranges words into contrast sets, meanwhile, has antonym pairs naturally arising where only two words are involved. By doing so, Murphy comments, it cannot "satisfactorily explain how binary opposition and non-binary contrasts can co-exist within the same semantic field", especially for the examples of emotion terms and color terms (Murphy 2000: 321–323).

Hence, against the view of words in a larger contrast set that can also be opposite, Murphy (2003) lists binarity as one of the nine properties in his restricting definition for semantic relations. Binarity here is referred to some relations that "relate only pairs of words, although larger sets of words may be semantically available for the relation (e.g., black/white rather than black/gray/white)" (2003: 26). He defines antonym relation by its binarity, since it is "rather similar to negation" (2003: 28).

But some later linguists present a different view on whether binarity is necessary in defining opposition. They can find a strong voice in the ones who holding the syntactic pattern approaches, for example, Mettinger (1994).

Interestingly, some of the later linguists, who hold the syntactic pattern approaches, also take the same view that only the binary pairs of contrast can be called opposite. Mettinger (1994), for example, thinks that the non-binary pairs "operate on the basis of semantic dimensions and semantic features", but can also be operated as "rank-terms", "degree-terms" or "grade-terms", according to their continuous scales and gradability.

Negation patterns are used to negate semantic feature(s) of some words, not the whole property of these words. The affirmed word is used to indicate the negated semantic feature(s) and further point out the affirmed feature(s). Since semantic features are not something binary, but multiple, so the words which can occur in negation patterns are not only opposite. On the other hand, there are only two positions in a pattern within a common negation pattern (at least the ones used in our experiment), it usually builds a binary relation between the two words and therefore makes the reading more like an opposite pairing. If we extended the experiment to a larger pattern, like '*bu4/not* a *bu4/not* b *bu4/not* c … *bu4* n but n + 1', the multiple relations will be more obvious.

5.5 Summary

In this chapter, we study how negation interacts with opposites in Chinese. We notice that words in negation frames are not equal to being opposites. Opposites with negation frames are used to emphasize the shared meaning of the negated part and affirmed part.

Moreover, negation frames can trigger out not only opposites, but also sub-events, synonyms, manners, attributes and paranyms. But the usages of negation frames for different semantic relational pairs are different. For manners, attributes and paranyms, the function is to make a choice between two candidates;

for sub-events, the negation patterns make a stop within a series of sub-events; and for near-synonyms, the negation patterns are pointing out the variation of two words in semantic features beyond conceptual meanings. In a word, the negation frames do not negate the whole semantic features of one word, but highlight some of its semantic features.

The result also suggests that negation frames do not require a binary pairing, but allow multiple choices for the same word. With the negation patterns, word pairs, like synonyms or paranyms, can be used as opposites in certain context.

Chapter 6
Conclusion

This study addresses two main questions based on three studies conducted Chinese opposites.

Firstly, how do we use opposites in Chinese?

1. On morphological level, the meaning of co-occurring opposites is decided by the construction (such as [A][−A], 大小 *da4/big xiao3/small,* "size") and the linking words (such as *from…to…*, 从大到小 *cong1/from da4/big dao4/to xiao3/small*, "from big to small" or "all sizes"). Together they identify a special domain or offer a eventual reading with the opposites (Sect. 3.4.1);
2. On discourse level, Chinese opposites share the same function categorization with English and Japanese, but the distributions of the three languages vary from each other. Coordinated Opposites and Ancillary Opposites are the most common functions in all three languages, but in English the percentages taken by the two categories are almost equal while in Chinese Coordinated Opposites are two times higher than that of Ancillary, and in Japanese, the situation is reverse to that of Chinese (Sect. 4.4.2);
3. In term of "canonicity", there are some opposite pairings, which are more frequently used in a wider range of syntactic frames, are called the "canonical" ones. Canonical pairings do not exist in some opposite concepts. Because for these concepts different pairings are used in different contexts and cannot be replaced by one other. Therefore none of them is widely used in discourses (Sect. 4.4.3);
4. Words in negation frames are not equal to opposites. Opposites with negation frames emphasize the overlapped meaning of the negated and affirmed parts. Negation frames would trigger out other semantic relations and the pragmatic function of these frames also changes with different relations. For example, with sub-events (看 *kan4/look* and 买 *mai3/buy*), the negation frame makes a stop in a series of actions (只看不买 *zhi3/only kan4/look bu4/not mai3/buy* "window shopping") (Sect. 5.4.2). This study also supports the hypothesis that opposites

J. Ding, *A Lexical Semantic Study of Chinese Opposites*,
Frontiers in Chinese Linguistics 1, https://doi.org/10.1007/978-981-10-6184-4_6

in language are not the same to logical negation (Sect. 5.4.1) and negation frames are not used only for binary relations (Sect. 5.4.3).

Secondly, how are sub-types of opposites (complementary, antonym and converse) used differently in Chinese?

1. On the morphological level, the order of pairing members of complementary and antonym is influenced by Pollyanna Principle and prosodic principle. But for converse pairs, temporal order is the crucial factor, since for words like 买 *mai3/buy* or 卖 *mai4/sell* it is hard to say which one is positive or negative. There are also cases, like 轻重 *qing1/light zhong4/heavy* and 难易 *nan1/difficult yi4/easy*, cannot be fully explained by above rules and the remain to be solved in later studies (Sect. 3.4.2);
2. On discourse level, the most commonly-used functions of antonym and converse opposites are Coordinated Opposites, Ancillary Opposite and Extreme Opposite, while for complementary opposites, Numeric Opposites, instead of Extreme Opposite, is one of the most common functions in usage. As a whole, the function distributions of antonym and converse are more similar to each other than that of complementary. It means more syntactic frames are shared by antonym and converse, with similar pragmatic usages, and for complementary opposites, the co-occurrence of them are used for different pragmatic meanings (Sect. 4.4.1);
3. Antonym and complementary pairs are more likely to have canonical pairings, while different contexts require different converse pairs and therefore it is harder for converse concepts to have canonical pairings. For all the three sub-types, it is more often to have syllabic matched pairings in Chinese data. Moreover, antonym and complementary pairs prefer to have mono-syllabic pairings, and converse pairs prefer to have bi-syllabic pairings (Sect. 4.4.3).

In this work, we study Chinese opposites to explore the characteristics of linguistic opposites. Chinese is a language relatively less explored in this area. The concept of "opposites" has been defined as an important semantic relation in early literatures but no compulsory or completed studies have been done on this topic of Chinese opposites. Compared with previous studies on similar topics, our research shows the following novel points:

a. A usage-based research to uncover the nature of opposites, which is long-time defined by meaning and context-contrast but not observed from morphological or discourse levels yet.
b. A larger sized corpus and the automatic extraction ensure the final result more convincing than that from case studies or manual selection;
c. Three related studies are designed from character-based level to discourse level, hence recover the full picture of opposites in a certain language (Chinese);
d. We explore the differences among complementary, antonym and converse, the three theoretically-discussed but practically-unexplored sub-types of opposites, therefore answer the question that how and why they vary from each other.

The results of this research question the theoretical discussion in previous studies from a practical aspect therefore offer readers a better understanding to the nature of Chinese opposites. The data we have is also useful in completing semantic relations of present lexical resources.

In this work, we employ syntactic frames to explore the behavior of opposites. And we also notice that, the pragmatic functions of these syntactic frames have influences on the semantic relation of the word pairings which occupy the frames. For example, a negation frame can generate a contrast reading within a synonym pairing. So, in our next research, it would be interesting to ask: how to make a new opposite pairing? Can it be constructed via pragmatic factors like syntactic frames, or via prosodic factors?

Appendix A
A Full List of Seed Pairings for Chinese Experiment on Fixed Words

上:下	余:缺	升:落	喜:悲	害:利	齐:乱	摘:戴	本:末	父:母
夫:妻	俗:雅	单:双	因:果	害:益	得:失	收:支	来:去	圆:方
东:西	俯:仰	南:北	土:洋	宽:窄	忙:闲	收:种	来:往	热:凉
进:出	借:还	香:臭	增:减	宽:严	快:钝	放:录	松:紧	热:冷
主:次	饿:饱	卸:装	增:删	密:疏	快:慢	放:捉	枯:荣	狭:广
主:宾	停:开	厌:喜	夏:冬	春:秋	急:慢	放:收	柔:刚	利:钝
主:客	偶:奇	厚:薄	夕:旦	黑:白	恨:爱	兴:灭	顶:底	生:死
乐:哀	入:出	顺:逆	外:里	富:穷	恩:仇	敌:友	欢:悲	生:熟
乐:悲	公:母	阴:晴	夜:日	富:贫	恶:善	中:外	正:反	瘪:饱
乖:淘	公:私	零:整	夜:昼	寡:多	惩:奖	聚:离	正:负	瘪:鼓
罪:功	内:外	脆:韧	大:小	对:错	君:臣	合:散	正:歪	起:落
乘:除	高:低	发:收	天:地	少:多	憎:爱	文:武	正:斜	盈:亏
买:卖	高:矮	受:施	违:奉	尾:首	成:败	邪:正	正:偏	阳:阴
苦:甘	净:脏	只:都	头:尾	巧:拙	抓:放	新:旧	此:彼	直:弯
系:解	罚:赏	右:左	奇:偶	巧:苯	拆:装	新:陈	死:活	直:曲
亡:存	尊:卑	情:理	奖:罚	进:退	那:这	新:老	求:供	省:费
亢:卑	减:添	同:异	女:男	差:好	拔:插	详:略	沉:浮	真:假
交:接	凶:吉	后:先	好:糟	干:湿	挖:填	无:有	沉:轻	真:伪
亮:暗	凹:凸	后:前	好:烂	幼:老	阔:穷	遮:露	还:借	睁:闭
亲:疏	分:合	吐:吞	好:坏	幼:长	挤:松	赔:赏	浊:清	败:赢
问:答	聚:散	吐:咽	好:歹	胖:瘦	授:领	早:晚	浑:清	碎:整
今:昔	利:弊	向:背	好:难	开:关	排:灌	早:迟	浓:淡	祸:福
今:古	简:繁	启:封	始:终	开:闭	接:送	旱:涝	精:粗	离:合
强:干	肥:瘦	吸:呼	存:取	开:合	长:短	明:暗	通:堵	婚:嫁
众:寡	加:减	和:差	学:教	开:封	接:断	易:难	涨:落	稀:密
纵:横	动:静	和:战	守:攻	张:合	推:拉	是:非	涩:滑	稀:稠
桀:棠	勤:懒	咽:吐	安:拆	张:驰	提:降	逮:放	深:浅	输:赢
伸:缩	化:冻	贩:卖	安:危	弱:强	插:拔	智:愚	添:减	迎:送

(continued)

J. Ding, *A Lexical Semantic Study of Chinese Opposites*,
Frontiers in Chinese Linguistics 1, https://doi.org/10.1007/978-981-10-6184-4

(continued)

胜:败	缓:急	赚:赔	实:虚	当:赎	揭:蒙	暑:寒	火:水	空:实
胜:负	升:降	喜:厌	荤:素	往:返	揭:贴	避:趋	灵:笨	穿:脱
竖:横	荣:辱	美:丑	舍:取	表:里	贬:褒	软:硬	谦:满	重:轻
笑:哭	红:白	老:少	苦:乐	衰:盛	购:销	贵:贱	退:入	野:朝
细:粗	纬:经	老:嫩	苦:甜	让:争	赎:当	贴:揭		

Appendix B
A Full List of Candidate Words in Each Conceptual Group

5 Complementary Pairs

alive&dead

活|生|存|活着|累活|活物|成活|回生|生还|生活|生存|在世|健在

死|亡|卒|逝|殁|殪|毙|殂|殒|薨|崩|殇|夭|殉|死亡|亡故|身故|物故|物化|去世|逝世|故世|谢世|弃世|过世|下世|凋谢|毙命|殒命|殒灭|殂谢|长逝|永诀|永别|长眠|故去|断气|咽气|合眼|闭眼|完蛋|呜呼|死去|辞世|已故|仙逝|千古|作古|归西|归天|过去|不讳|病故|病逝|牺牲|舍身|献身|就义|捐躯|殉职|殉国|殉难|殉节|效死|效命|授命|阵亡|横死|凶死|丧命|送命|毙命|暴卒|没命|丧生|身亡|丧身|饿死|升天|坐化|羽化|物化|圆寂|夭折|夭亡|早逝|成仁|死物|伤亡|坏死|瘐死|击毙

male&female

雄|公|牡|男|乾|阳|男|子|君|郎|哥|汉|士|红男|男人|男子|男儿|汉子|丈夫|官人|须眉|壮汉|男士|爷儿|爷们|先生|男性|小先生|男人家|光身汉|男子汉|兄|哥|昆|兄长|哥哥|阿哥|长兄|大哥|家兄|胞兄|弟|棣|弟弟|兄弟|阿弟|令弟|胞弟|夫|郎|丈夫|男人|先生|老公|汉子|人夫|爷们|郎君|官人|良人|夫子|夫君|夫婿|相公|当家的|老头子|子|儿|崽|子嗣|小子|庶子|爱子|小儿|犬子|令郎|少爷|相公|公子|哥儿|亲子|儿子

雌|母|牝|草|女|坤|阴|娘|妇|士女|绿女|小姐|仕女|太太|夫人|贵妇|贱人|祸水|巧妇|村姑|娘们|妞儿|少妇|婆娘|婆姨|娘子|姑娘|少女|丫头|千金|闺女|室女|姑子|女流|才女|女郎|巾帼|红装|女人|女子|女性|女士|女儿|妇女|妇道|妇人|女性|少奶奶|贵妇人|女人家|大姑娘|小姑娘|老姑娘|春姑娘|小娘子|半边天|娘子军|姐|姊|阿姐|姐姐|老姐儿|师姐|妹|娣|阿妹|妹妹|妹子|胞妹|小妹|师妹|妻|内|媳妇|妻子|爱人|妻室|夫人|女人|老婆|太太|婆娘|婆姨|娘们|娘子||内助|妻妾|爱妻|内人|拙荆|屋里|发妻|雌老虎|贤内助|老婆子|囡|丫|妮|爱女|小女|令爱|千金|女儿|闺女|姑娘|丫头|幼女

opposite=true&false

实|真|诚|诚实|忠实|实际|实在|笃实|真正|真性|真格|真真|真实|确凿|凿凿|无疑|的确|确切|真切|逼真|翔实|可靠|有据|确实|属实|如实|真确|真心实意|诚心诚意|实事求是|真人真事|动真格的|货真价实|原汁原味|地地道道|名副其实|有名有实|名不虚传|名下无虚|真名实姓|耳闻目睹|有目共睹|有凭有据|有案可稽|千真万确|无可置疑|毋庸置疑|不容置疑|铁案如山|实实在在|真真切切|无可辩驳|
无可争议|确确实实|毋庸讳言|毋庸置言|铁证如山

虚|假|伪|赝|幻|虚伪|冒牌|仿真|搀假|虚假|名义|挂名|假想|假设|虚设|虚设|子虚|虚妄|无稽|荒诞|夸诞|假冒伪劣|子虚乌有|有名无实|名过其实|名不副实|名存实

J. Ding, *A Lexical Semantic Study of Chinese Opposites*,
Frontiers in Chinese Linguistics 1, https://doi.org/10.1007/978-981-10-6184-4

亡|虚有其表|徒有虚名|言过其实|南箕北斗|假门假事|假眉三道|形同虚设|名难副实|其实难副|名不符实|言不由衷|心口不一|言行不一|表里不一|荒诞不经

open&close
开|启|展|敞|打开|张开|敞开|拉开|启封|翻开|开启|开门|开闸
关|闭|合|掩|阖|密闭|虚掩|关掉|闭合|封关|闭锁|关门|关闭

even&odd
双|偶|对|复|俪|骈|偶数|双数|对偶|双料|双双|对仗
单|孤|独|寡|单瓣|奇数|单数

12 Antonym Pairs

fast&slow
快|速|疾|飞|急|迅|迅疾|急速|急性|急遽|急剧|急骤|急促|湍急|急湍|加急|疾速|快速|高速|迅速|神速|迅猛|火速|飞速|全速|迅捷|敏捷|矫捷|便捷|轻捷|迅疾|麻利|快当|飞快|飞跃|灵通|劈手|很快|快快|霎时|高效|快捷|如梭|跌进|速成|疾驰|急湍湍|一溜烟|短平快|不会儿|腾云驾雾|骨腾肉飞|风驰电掣|追风逐电|一日千里|日行千里|光阴似箭|日月如梭|不胫而走|不翼而飞|急转直下|一泻千里|稍纵即逝|眼捷手快|兵贵神速|不假思索|一目十行|一挥而就|一蹴而就|指日可待|计日程功|飞针走线|急若流星
慢|缓|徐|缓慢|舒缓|款款|徐徐|迟迟|磨蹭|迂缓|迟缓|迟延|迟滞|悠悠|冉冉|慢性|缓缓|减缓|暂缓|放缓|慢悠悠 |慢腾腾|慢吞吞|慢慢吞吞|慢慢悠悠|蜗行牛步|慢慢腾腾|慢条斯理|磨磨蹭蹭

light&dark
亮|明|皓|煌|晔|灿|炳|焕|炯|杲|烁|熠|煊|灼|朗|明亮|亮堂|通亮|光亮|雪亮|鲜亮|敞亮|豁亮|透亮|清亮|明朗|清明|通明|鲜明|光明|透亮|辉煌|明快|黑亮|银亮|锃亮|灼亮|空明|有光|耀眼|夺目|炫目|刺眼|灿烂|粲然|璀璨|耀目|炯炯|灼灼|皎洁|皎皎|熠熠|光洁|晶莹|晶亮|明澈|亮泽|荧荧|熹微|微亮|油光|贼亮|金灿灿|亮光光|亮闪闪|亮铮铮|亮堂堂|光灿灿|亮晃晃|亮亮的|红灿灿|明晃晃|亮晶晶|水汪汪|蒙蒙亮|麻麻亮|油汪汪|火光烛天|光芒万丈|光辉灿烂|心明眼亮|灯火辉煌|灿若云霞|灿若群星|群星璀璨|璀璨夺目|光彩耀目|炯炯有神|熠熠生辉|皓月当空|月明如镜|月光如水|秋月当空|光彩照人
暗|昧|森|黑|阴暗|幽暗|晦暗|昏暗|灰暗|黯淡|暗淡|阴沉|昏沉|昏黄|黯然|惨淡|惨白|背阴|背光|朦胧|幽幽|幽然|黑暗|昏黑|黝黑|黢黑|墨黑|漆黑|麻麻黑|暗沉沉|阴森森|毒花花|灰沉沉|黑沉沉|灰蒙蒙|黑糊糊|黑黝黝|黑洞洞|黑咕隆咚|黑灯瞎火|漆黑一团|黑咕隆冬|天昏地暗|昏天黑地

strong&weak
佶|健|壮|强|劲|雄|精|稳固|牢固|坚固|巩固|坚实|结实|深厚|强压|强盛|富强|不衰|稳步|坚牢|雄强|根深蒂固|深根固蒂|坚不可摧|坚如磐石|稳如泰山|固若金汤|金城汤池|牢不可破|壁垒森严|钢铁长城|铜墙铁壁|铁打江山|长盛不衰|兵强马壮|所向无敌|所向披靡|一往无前|无往不胜|无坚不摧|攻无不克|战无不胜|泰山压顶|摧枯拉朽|降龙伏虎|兵不血刃|投鞭断流|人多势众|切实有力|船坚炮利|国富民强|繁荣富强|国富民安|民富国强|富国强兵
孱|弱|虚|矫|弱|软|弱小|软弱|薄弱|虚弱|单弱|衰弱|微弱|贫弱|柔弱|衰微|单薄|势单力薄|不堪一击|一触即溃|赤手空拳|手无寸铁|立足未稳|一虎势单|身单力薄

big&small

大|巨|宏|硕|庞|肥|巨大|硕大|庞大|宏大|偌大|粗大|高大|洪大|极大|特大|宽大|肥大|大型|巨型|重型|超大|大幅度|特大型|重特大|硕大无朋|庞然大物|翻天覆地|大而无当|硕大无比

小|微|细|纤|芾|微小|细小|微细|细微|幽微|纤维|纤毫|纤小|短小|矮小|蝇头|小型|微型|袖珍|小小|很小|不大|最小|小小的|小口径|一丁点儿|小不点儿|微乎其微

wide&narrow

宽|敞|广|泛|宽敞|宽阔|宽大|宽广|宽绰|宽舒|宽余|阔大|广泛|广阔|宽广|广大|宽泛|普遍|轩敞|坦荡|开豁|开阔|开朗|放宽|宽旷|宽心|拓宽|平阔|无穷|无限|无边|无际|宽宽敞敞|坦坦荡荡|漫无止境|无边无际|无穷无尽|海阔天空|漫无边际|漫无际涯|一望无涯

窄|狭|褊|蹙|陋|瘦|仄|隘|狭窄|狭小|窄窄|窄小|褊狭|局促|狭隘|逼仄|湫隘|偏狭|小心眼儿

good&bad

好|优|精|良|帅|佳|美|妙|良好|大好|优良|精良|优秀|优异|精彩|出色|绝妙|漂亮|精美|美好|完美|美妙|精粹|精练|优质|上好|上上|理想|可以|地道|可观|不错|要得|好好|拔尖|佳绩|出彩|上佳|甚佳|醇美|不含糊|了不起|呱呱叫|顶呱呱|够味儿|好生生|说得着|过得硬|名特优|尽如人意|完美无缺|尽善尽美|十全十美|白璧无瑕|妙不可言|名不虚传|有目共赏|有口皆碑|口碑载道|脍炙人口|交口称誉|得天独厚|完好无损|有滋有味|两全其美|名特优新

坏|差|次|软|破|糟|鬼|赖|孬|莠|劣|恶|歹|不好|不良|不行|不妙|不善|差劲|稀松|糟糕|蹩脚|涂鸦|窳劣|次等|欠佳|不成|二流|次于|恶劣|低劣|粗劣|卑劣|拙劣|猥陋|卑下|劣质|伪劣|恶性|歹心|假劣|二五眼|差点儿|不成话|要不得|一团糟|不足取|不像话|驴鸣狗吠|一无可取|一塌糊涂|看不上眼|不堪设想

thick&thin

浓|厚|稠|糨|黏|腻|糯|厚实|丰厚|粗厚|厚厚|浓重|浓厚|浓浓|粘稠|黏糊|厚实实|厚厚的|厚墩墩|浓浓的|油腻腻|稠乎乎

薄|稀|淡|稀薄|淡薄|单薄|超薄|稀溜溜|淡淡的|薄薄的

cold&hot

冷|寒|冰|凉|冻|清寒|寒冷|冰冷|冰凉|阴冷|僵冷|寒湿|发潮|苦寒|严寒|高寒|冷峭|寒峭|刺骨|惨烈|干冷|凄清|凛凛|凛冽|春寒|料峭|奇寒|饥寒|冷飕飕|冷丝丝|冷溲溲|冷冰冰|寒气袭人|天寒地冻|滴水成冰|冰天雪地|冰冻三尺|春寒料峭|寒风料峭|寒意料峭|饥寒交加|冷若冰霜

热|烫|炎|燠|炽|暑|热火|热和|热乎|滚烫|滚热|灼热|热力|温热|余热|炎热|炎炎|暑热|炽热|火热|酷热|酷暑|燥热|熏蒸|溽暑|热乎乎|热烘烘|热腾腾|热滚滚|热哄哄|热呼呼|火辣辣|热辣辣|骄阳似火|汗流浃背|汗如雨下|铄石流金|流金铄石|烈日当空

expensive&cheap

俯|垂|贵|尊|稚|玉|华|大|宝|钧|惠|珍|尊贵|高贵|显贵|贵重|名贵|宝贵|可贵|华贵|珍贵|珍奇|珍异|金玉|难得|无价|珍稀|不菲|昂贵|腾贵|高昂|值钱|有头有脸|高不可攀|惟它独尊|难能可贵|弥足珍贵|奇货可居|价值连城|价值千金||一刻千金|寸土寸金|寸草寸金|米珠薪桂|质次价高

贱|廉|卑|微|低|低贱|卑微|微贱|轻贱|贫贱|下贱|卑微|低微|低下|卑下|卑鄙|寒微|便宜|低廉|廉价|价廉|低价|质优价廉|价廉质优|低人一等|低三下四|人微言轻|惠而不费|价廉物美|物美价廉

fat&slim

粗|侉|奘|阔|胖|肥|腴|短粗|肥胖|肥壮|肥硕|肥实|肥厚|丰满|丰盈|丰腴|充盈|丰润|胖胖|臃肿|虚胖|粗大|肥大|粗壮|粗实|粗重|心广体胖|心宽体胖|肥得鲁儿|膀阔腰圆|膘肥肉厚|大腹便便|脑满肠肥|五大三粗

瘦|细|清瘦|消瘦|清癯|瘦小|瘦瘠|干瘪|枯瘦|瘦干|瘦削|干瘦|黑瘦|精瘦|憔悴|枯槁|纤细|细小|纤小|细长|苗条|细弱|亘细|细部|细高|细细|骨瘦如柴|骨头架子|瘦骨嶙峋|黄皮寡瘦|面黄肌瘦|鸠形鹄面

beautiful&ugly

美|丽|俏|娟|绮|妍|艳|娇|绚|婷|俊|菲菲|美美|幽美|泛美|姣好|秀美|秀气|清秀|灵秀|挺秀|娟秀|韶秀|秀丽|明丽|俏丽|奇秀|脆丽|秀色|华丽|富丽|壮丽|绮丽|瑰丽|艳丽|亮丽|壮伟|鲜艳|浓艳|妖艳|明媚|秀媚|妩媚|美艳|绚丽|绚烂|烂漫|灿烂|妖艳|妖冶|妖媚|妖娆|娇媚|柔媚|娇娆|娇艳|多姿|锦绣|入画|旖旎|美貌|标致|体面|上相|柔美|冶容|秀雅|绰约|婵娟|娟娟|窈窕|绝色|姣妍|婷婷|俊美|俊秀|俊俏|俏皮|英俊|堂堂|翩翩|袅娜|婀娜|娉婷|亭亭|美丽|漂亮|好看|受看|中看|入眼|顺眼|悦目|美观|华美|优美|美妙|嫣然|千娇百媚|柔情绰态|娇艳欲滴|虬曲挺秀|钟灵毓秀|花枝招展|如花似锦|光彩夺目|鲜艳夺目|万紫千红|姹紫嫣红|花团锦簇|琳琅满目|美不胜收|多姿多彩|繁花似锦|分外夺目|光灿夺目|灿烂夺目|绚丽夺目|灿若云霞|灿若星河|光芒四射|山明水秀|风景如画|花香鸟语|山青水秀|华章锦绣|眉清目秀|堂堂正正|一表人才|明眸皓齿|冰肌玉骨|花容玉貌|秀外慧中|闭月羞花|沉鱼落雁|国色天香|天香国色|天姿国色|倾国倾城|佳妙无双|倾城倾国|绝世无匹|西装革履|阳刚之美|楚楚静立|眉清目朗|楚楚动人|风华绝代|美若天仙|如花似玉|袅袅婷婷|仪态万方|亭亭玉立|绰约多姿

丑|陋|猥|丑陋|难看|寒碜|猥琐|其貌不扬|面目可憎|龇牙咧嘴|贼眉鼠眼|獐头鼠目|见不得人|人老珠黄

clever&foolish

智|睿|神|灵|快|聪|急智|能干|灵气|能者|早慧|融智|精明|灵动|趁机|英明|明智|睿智|精明|机智|机灵|机敏|机警|灵巧|灵敏|灵活|精灵|玲珑|机巧|乖巧|乖觉|敏锐|锐敏|敏感|伶俐|聪明|聪慧|明慧|智慧|聪颖|颖悟|灵性|颖慧|慧黠|内秀|明白|聪敏|颖慧|小聪明|敏锐性|秀外慧中|耳聪目明|足智多谋|大智若愚|生财有道|有头有脑|聪明伶俐|大巧若拙|多谋善断|过目不忘|过目成诵|一目十行|才思敏捷|英名盖世|料事如神|独具只眼|明察秋毫|见微知著|金睛火眼|随机应变|临机应变|通权达变|便宜行事|见机行事|手急眼快|相机行事|牙白口清|眼捷手快|人杰地灵|能屈能伸|千伶百俐|聪明伶俐|耳听八方|能进能出

笨|拙|痴|蠢|愚|傻|懵|呆|愚笨|笨拙|拙笨|迂拙|愚蠢|愚笨|愚拙|愚鲁|愚昧|痴呆|呆笨|粗笨|傻气|不灵|蠢笨|蠢物|愚钝|弱智|发蒙|蒙昧|懵懂|颟顸|糊涂|悖晦|昏庸|昏聩|胡涂|鲁钝|迟钝|顽钝|驽钝|呆笨|木讷|讷讷|呆傻|傻呵呵|傻乎乎|傻劲儿|昏昏然|马大哈|呆愣愣|痴呆呆|呆呆地|傻里傻气|愚不可及|愚昧无知|昏头转向|买椟还珠|骑马找马|缺心眼儿|舍珠买椟|糊里糊涂|稀里糊涂|昏头昏脑|浑头浑脑|晕头转向|蒙头转向|迷迷糊糊|如堕烟海|如坐云雾|当局者迷|聪明一世|呆头呆脑|张口结舌|笨口拙舌|笨手笨脚|木雕泥塑|泥塑木雕|木头疙瘩|怯头怯脑

5 Converse Pairs

buy&sell

买|购|置|贩|进|赎|趸|订|购买|购置|置备|置办|采购|采办|购入|购得|买入|选购|购进|买进|进货|收购|收买|买断|收订|购回|订购|定购|订货|定货|预购|预订|订座|订阅|邮购|函购|竞买|征购|统购|认购|赊购|套购|抢购|争购|求购|申购|并购|承购|代购|乱购|回购|添置|赎买||续订|征订|抢购一空
卖|售|沽|鬻|销|榷|抛|粜|出卖|贩卖|出售|发售|售卖|趸售|倒卖|倒腾|购销|倒手|销售|销行|行销|售货|兜销|兜售|推销|经售|经销|专卖|抛售|返销|批发|发行|批零|批销|联销|零售|零卖|寄卖|寄售|拍卖|甩卖|处理|出倒|招盘|出盘|出让|转让|变卖|脱手|出脱|出手|出粜|炒卖|卖掉|卖出|售出|制售|军售|卖给|送货|拐卖|义卖|转卖|典卖|贱卖|盗卖|叫卖|摊售|配售|代售|搭售|预售|交售|内销|外销|畅销|滞销|包销|代销|赊销|倾销|统销|供销|还销|展销|俏销|旺销|调销|冲销|承销|促销|适销|远销|产销|分销|自销|传销|直销|营销|练摊|摆售|出摊|销货|有偿|待价而沽|自产自销|有奖销售|炒买炒卖|有偿转让

teach&study

诲|育|传|授|引|导|教育|教导|教化|感化|教诲|训诲|训迪|启蒙|施教|育才|传艺|宣教|胎教|劳教|身教|言教|传授|相传|灌输|授受|真传|口授|面授|函授|示范|示例|演示|开导|诱导|启发|启示|启迪|诱发|发蒙|启蒙|指点|指导|点拨|点化|唤醒|唤起|提醒|提拔|提示|引导|指引|导诊|辅导|引向|导向|导引|春风化雨|耳提面命|寓教于乐|化雨春风|有教无类|谆谆教导|循循善诱|诲人不倦|谆谆教诲|安居乐教|因材施教|口传心授|衣钵相传|面授机宜|以身作则|言传身教|现身说法|为人师表|发聋振聩|抛砖引玉|因势利导|指点迷津|安居而乐教|桃李满天下|身教胜于言教
读|念|学|习|攻|修|仿|摹|效|拟|学学|复习|温习|温课|复课|温书|同窗|自学|自习|自修|进修|实习|见习|留学|留洋|学习|念书|读书|上学|就学|求学|修业|攻读|深造|入学|求艺|初学|学法|研习|预习|旁听|借读|补习|研读|主修|辅修|研修|重修|必修|选修|学艺|学步|学到|学好|在读|从师|投师|拜师|受业|就读|师从|模仿|效仿|仿效|模拟|仿照|取法|师法|效法|宪章|祖述|踵武|学舌|因袭|依傍|效尤|摹仿|熟记|取长补短|用长避短|囫囵吞枣|生吞活剥|不求甚解|学无止境|艺无止境|死记硬背|东施效颦|邯郸学步|鹦鹉学舌|照猫画虎|如法炮制|人云亦云|亦步亦趋|拾人牙慧|上行下效|照葫芦画瓢|依样画葫芦|上梁不正下梁歪

come&go

来|莅|来到|到来|过来|开来|飞来|前来|来临|驶来|赶到|赶来|莅临|降临|惠临|光临|驾临|贲临|亲临|光顾|惠顾|屈驾|慕名而来|不期而至|翩然而至|乘兴而来|远道而来|随之而来|接踵而来|源源而来|纷至沓来|蜂拥而来|接踵而至|席卷而来
去|往|奔|赴|趸|前往|前去|过去|通往|转赴|开往|开赴|奔赴|赶赴|赶往|此行|分赴|直奔|一怒而去|拂袖而去|拂衣而去|扬长而去

receive&give

得|取|获|抱|博|落|沾|夺|牟|渔|取得|得到|获得|博得|赢得|获取|博取|收获|到手|拿走|查获|得出|汲取|得来|应得|荣获|荣膺|捧得|喜获|荣立|争取|争得|力争|分得|夺取|夺得|牟取|谋取|拿到|力求|所得|吸取|摄取|截取|换取|猎取|掠取|窃取|诈取|智取|赚取|读取|抽取|套取|调取|撷取|争光|争当|夺金|得分|兼得|垂手而得|垂手可得|失而复得|合浦还珠|牟取暴利|立等可取|一举多得
扔|抛|废|弃|委|丢|摈|舍|抛弃|摈弃|捐弃|丢弃|废弃|撇弃|屏弃|毁弃|遗弃|废除|丢掉|撇开|撇下|闲弃|摒弃|抛开|剥弃|舍弃|放弃|割舍|割爱|扬弃|舍去|舍命|弃权|忍痛割爱|挥之即去

offer&accept

馈|赠|饩|赍|贻|送|遗|给|赏|赐|贶|赠送|馈送|奉送|馈赠|捐赠|赠与|赠给|赠予|转送|转赠|送礼|陪送|回礼|还礼|回赠|赏赐|赐予|天赐|赠机|受赠|敬献|敬赠|追赠|恩赐
受|领|禀|奉|膺|纳|接受|领受|收受|承受|经受

Appendix C
Examples for Each Chinese Syntactic Frames

Ancillary Opposite

noun be A, noun be –A: 搞经济心要热,脑要冷;风是凉的,情是热的
noun A, noun –A: 假集体,真个体; 个子小能量大; 规模大负债率低
A noun, –A noun: 淡了过年气氛,浓了春耕生产热情; 重口味、轻营养; 肥了地方、瘦了国家
(be) A like noun, (be) –A like: 粗如大缸、细如牛毛
noun (be) more A, noun (be) more –A: 冰山愈冷情愈热; 天越黑它越亮
verb A noun, verb –A noun: 江总书记强调抓好大型,放开放活小型

Coordinated Opposite

A and –A: 实施小私有化和大私有化方案; 今天的人吃了细还想粗
(be) A like noun, (be) –A like noun: 小至电池,大到照相机
verb A, verb –A: 顶酷暑,冒严寒; 知冷知热
no matter A or –A: 全连官兵无论身体强弱胖瘦; 国家不分大、小,强、弱,贫、富
not only A, but also –A: 不光是卖不难,买也不难; 不论穷国富国
A but also –A: 荒诞而又真实的故事

Comparative Opposite

more A than –A: 好多于差
less A than –A: 男少于女

Distinguished Opposite

sometimes A sometimes B时热时冷
A one year, –A one year: 贵一年、贱一年
A –A fan3cha1/contrast:冷热反差
A and –A bu4yi1/different: 高低不一
A –A zhi1/DE fen1/disparity: 保安有“真”“假”之分

J. Ding, *A Lexical Semantic Study of Chinese Opposites*,
Frontiers in Chinese Linguistics 1, https://doi.org/10.1007/978-981-10-6184-4

Transitional Opposite

first A then –A: 先急后缓; 前快后慢
from A to –A: 由弱趋强; 林场由小到大
Negated Opposite
(be) A not (be) –A: 宜快不宜慢
verb A, not verb –A (verb1=verb2): 要贵的不要贱的

Extreme Opposite

the most A be…, the most –A be: 亚洲消费最昂贵的城市是日本东京, 物价最便宜的是印度孟买; 最高温度可以达到摄氏四十多度,最低的也有 十几度
A (be)…, –A (be)…: 快则三年多,慢则十几年; 大的有250平方米, 小的只有几十平方米; 厚的有20米, 最薄的只有0.2米

Numeric Opposite

number A number –A: 两大一小

Others

yi3/use A dui4/counterforce –A:以慢对快
yi3/use A jian4/speculate –A: 以小见大 (“the child is father of the man”)
half A half –A: 半死不活;
bu4/not A bu4/not –A: 不高不低
A verb –A: 大欺小

References

(In English)

Cann, R. 1993. *Formal semantics: An introduction*. Cambridge: Cambridge University Press.

Cann, R. 2002. Descriptive models for sense relations III: Formal Semantics: 549–555. In *Handbook of Lexicology*, ed. D.A. Cruse, F. Huandsnurcher, M. Job, and P.R. Lutzeier, 498–508. Berlin: de Gruyter.

Cann, R. 2011. Sense relations. In *Semantics* (HSK 33.1), ed. Maienborn, von Heusinger and Portner, 456–479. Berlin: De Gruyter.

Chinese Knowledge Information Processing Group (CKIP). 1993. Chinese word classes. *CKIP Technical Report No. 93-05*. Taipei: Academia Sinica.

Croft, W., and D.A. Cruse. 2004. *Cognitive linguistics*. Cambridge: Cambridge University Press.

Cruse, D.A. 1986. *Lexical semantics*. Cambridge: Cambridge University Press.

Cruse, D.A. 1994. Prototype theory and lexical relations. *Rivista di linguisitca* 6: 167–188.

Cruse, D.A. 2004. *Meaning in language: An introduction to semantics and pragmatics*, 2nd ed. New York: Oxford University Press.

Cruse, D.A. 2006. *A glossary of semantics and pragmatics*. Edinburgh: Edinburgh University Press.

Deese, J. 1964. The associative structure of some common English adjectives. *Journal of Verbal Learning and Verbal Behaviour* 3: 347–357.

Ding, J., and C.-R. Huang. 2012. Negation and double negation. In *Proceedings of Chinese lexical semantics workshop*, CLSW 2012, ed. Ji, D., and G.Xiao, 736–744. Heidelberg: Springer.

Ding, J., and C.-R. Huang. 2013. Markedness of opposite. In *Proceedings of Chinese lexical semantics workshop*, CLSW 2013, ed. Liu, P., and Q. Su, 191–195. Heidelberg: Springer.

Ding, J., and C.-R. Huang. 2014. Word ordering in Chinese opposite compounds. In *Proceedings of Chinese lexical semantics workshop*, CLSW 2014, ed. Su, X., and T. He, 12–20. Heidelberg: Springer.

Geeraerts, D. 2002. Conceptual approaches III: Prototype theory. In *Handbook of lexicology*, ed. Cruse, D.A., F. Hundsnurscher, M. Job, and P.-R. Lutzeier, 284–291. Berlin: De Gruyter.

Herrmann, D.J., R. Chaffin, M.P. Daniel, and R.S. Wool. 1986. The role of elements of relation definition in antonym and synonym comprehension. *Zeitschrift fur Psychologie* 194: 133–153.

Jones, S. 2002. *Antonymy: A corpus-based perspective*. London: Routledge.

Johns, S. 2006. A Lexico-syntactic analysis of antonym co-occurrence in spoken English. *Text & Talk* 26–2: 191–216.

Jones, S., and M.L. Murphy. 2005. Using corpora to investigate antonym acquisition. *International Journal of Corpus Linguistics* 10: 401–422.

J. Ding, *A Lexical Semantic Study of Chinese Opposites*,
Frontiers in Chinese Linguistics 1, https://doi.org/10.1007/978-981-10-6184-4

Jones, S., C. Paradis, M.L. Murphy, and C. Willners. 2007. Googling for 'Opposites': A web-based study of antonym canonicity. *Corpora* 2 (2): 129–154.

Jones, S., M.L. Murphy, C. Paradis, and C. Willners. 2012. *Antonyms in English: Construals, constructions and canonicity*. Cambridge: Cambridge University Press.

Lehrer, A., and K. Lehrer. 1982. Antonymy. *Linguistics and Philosophy* 5: 483–501.

Lehrer, A. 1985. Markedness and antonymy. *Linguistics* 21: 397–429.

Lyons, J. 1968. *Introduction to theoretical linguistics*. Cambridge: Cambridge University Press.

Lyons, J. 1977. *Semantics*, vol. 1. Cambridge: Cambridge University Press.

Manfred, Krifka. 2007. Negated antonyms: Creating and filling the gap. In *Presupposition and implicature in compositional semantics (Palgrave Studies in Pragmatics, Language and Cognition)*, ed. Uli Sauerland and Penka Stateva, 163–177. Basingstoke and New York: Palgrave Macmillan.

Matlin, M.W., and D.J. Stang. 1978. *The pollyanna principle: Selectivity in language, memory, and thought*. Cambridge, MA: Schenkman Publishing.

Mettinger, A. 1994. *Aspects of semantic opposition in English*. Oxford: Clarendon Press.

Miller, G.A., and C. Fellbaum. 1991. Semantic networks of English. *Cognition* 41: 197–229.

Muehleisen, V., and M. Isono. 2009. Antonymous adjectives in Japanese discourse. *Journal of Pragmatics* 41: 2185–2203.

Murphy, M.L. 2000. Knowledge of words versus knowledge about words: The conceptual basis of lexical relations. In *The lexicon/encyclopedia interface*, ed. Bert Peeters, 317–348. Amsterdam: Elsevier.

Murphy, M.L. 2003. *Semantic relations and the lexicon: Antonyms, synonyms and other semantic paradigms*. Cambridge: Cambridge University Press.

Murphy, M.L., and S. Jones. 2008. Antonyms in children's and child-directed speech. *First Language* 28: 403–430.

Palmer, F.R. 1981. *Semantics: A new outline*, 2nd ed. Cambridge: Cambridge University Press.

Paradis, C. 2005. Ontologies and construals in lexical semantics. *Axiomaches* 15: 541–573.

Paradis, C., C. Willners, S. Löhndorf, and M.L. Murphy. 2006. Quantifying aspects of antonym canonicity in English and Swedish: Textual and experimental. *Presented at quantitative investigations in theoretical linguistics* 2, Osnabrück, Germany, 1–2 June.

Paradis, C., C. Willners, M.L. Murphy, and S. Jones. 2009. Good and bad opposites: Using textual and experimental techniques to measure canonicity. *The Mental Lexicon* 4 (3): 380–429.

Paradis, C. 2010. Good, better and superb antonyms: A conceptual construal approach. In *The annual of texts by foreign guest professors*. Faculty of Philosophy and Arts, Charles University in Prague.

Waugh, L.R. 1982. Marked and unmarked: A choice between unequals. *Semiotica* 38: 299–318.

Willners, C., and C. Paradis. 2010. Swedish opposites: A multi-method approach to 'goodness of antonymy'. In *Lexical-semantic relations*, ed. Petra Storjohann, 15–48. John Benjamins Publishing.

Zwicky, A. 1978. On markedness in morphology. *Die Sprache* 24: 129–143.

(In Chinese)

Chen, A., and P. Yu. 1979. Word order of bisyllabic compounds. *Zhongguo Yuwen* 2.
Fu, H. 1996. *Chinese lexicology*, 4th ed. Hefei: Anhui Education Press.
He, G., et al. (eds.). 2005. *Dictionary of opposite in modern Chinese*. Shanghai: Shanghai Lexicographical Publishing House.
Jiang, S. 2000. *A collection of studying history for lexicology and syntax in Chinese*. Beijing: Commercial Press.
Sheng, S. 1958. *Notes on word with opposite meaning*. *Chinese studies*, vol. 3.
Shi, A., and R. Zhan. 1983. Antonym: common features, sub-types and unbalance. *Anthology on Linguistics* 10.
Tang, T.-C. 1979. *Studies on Chinese morphology and syntax*. Taipei: Taiwan Student Book Press.
Xu, W. 2000. *Chinese lexicology in 20th century*. Taiyuan: Booksea Publisher.
Zhang, Q. (ed.). 2009. *Dictionary of opposite*. Shanghai: Shanghai Dictionary Publisher.
Zhou, Z. 1985. Chinese bisyllabic compounds and tones. *Journal of Peking University (Philosophy & Social Sciences)* 3.

The manufacturer's authorised representative in the EU is Springer
Nature Customer Service Centre GmbH, Europaplatz 3, 69115 Heidelberg,
Germany. If you have any concerns regarding our products, please
contact ProductSafety@springernature.com

Printed and bound by CPI Group (UK) Ltd, Croydon, CR0 4YY
01/10/2026
02225883-0007